REFLECTIONS OF A DINOSAUR PRIEST

Why Squares Can't be Circled

By
James B. Lloyd, CSP, PhD

Appropriate Press

Table of Contents

Celibacy! Consecrated Chastity! Is It for Cold-Blooded, Unaffectionate Schizoids?

I am a Catholic priest. For over fifty years I have been a priest. I am dedicated and vowed to celibacy and consecrated chastity. Over those fifty years, literally hundreds of persons have, by innuendo, indirection or outright allegation, challenged or questioned me about my sanity, my sexual balance or my inanity—in relation to celibacy. I have been asked: "How can anyone live without an active sexual life?" Surely, they say, celibacy has to make a person unbalanced. (Obviously, there are persons who are celibate who belong in mental hospitals for reasons other than celibacy.)

The message which has come across to me was that anyone so distorted as to take a vow of celibacy—for whatever reason—must be terribly cold about human love. Such a person must be flat emotionally and certainly sexually repressed. Celibates must be distant, eggheaded and heavily involved in cerebral pursuits. Celibates must work it off by gardening, beekeeping or obsessive screaming on protest, lines outside abortion mills. Male celibates surely must, if not hate women, view females as unattractive, undesirable, useless or uninteresting with the possible exceptions of quasi-maids, secretaries or surrogate mothers.

Celibacy, as outlined above, leads, I have been told, for both men and women into fornication, adultery, porno, pedophilia, masturbation, homosexuality and—for males—into fear of the opposite sex. As the hip generation sees it—if only these poor, deluded chastity people had what street wisdom calls healthy sexuality, the above-mentioned sexual difficulties would disappear or at least be attenuated.

The highly publicized sexual scandals of the past decade could hardly have happened, they say, if Gen X values were taught and lived. It is all traceable to this crazy, outmoded idea of celibacy. How does a celibate respond to this challenge?

The description outlined above baffles me. I, as a celibate of more than half a century, with thousands more like me, am astounded at the superficial observations of what I would have called knowledgeable and educated people.

Study after study has shown that the real link between the sorry, sick litany listed above is not a married state or an unmarried state. It is self-image. It is not sexual experience or a lack of sexual experience which is the powerful determinant. It is self-concept. It is how we feel and think about ourselves. To jump on celibacy as if it were the only factor for deviation is to drag into the framework a very large red herring. Does Gen X know that, according to the study from Emory University, eighty percent of all crimes involving pedophilia were done by married men? That these men would have committed these crimes even if they were celibate? Problems come not from sexual or non-sexual experience per se! They come from identity—way-down-deep identity.

Afraid of girls? Dislike girls? I (and the thousands of other celibates) can't identify with such weird and unnatural sentiments. I remember being in love (defined as being smitten by the beauty and charm of girls) with so many females in my lifetime. Start with the fourth grade and Marie Becker who was my girl at that time. In high school, I was the local Romeo.

Even when I was twelve and highly skilled in dancing the Lindy, Bunny Hug and the Shag, I flirted with girls outrageously. I had a Vaudeville background as well as a generous Jewish cousin named Irwin who gave me his old jacket with huge, padded shoulders. With such a formidable array of equipment, I would charm giggling young girls. Once, as I so behaved, a jealous classmate, Jackie Weir, grabbed the shoulders and shouted: "Look, girls, they're fake." Even at that age, I, the future celibate, liked females.

I fondly remember my college girlfriend, Dolly Laura Stock, who was reputedly the best-looking girl in the parish and a terrific dancer—if not too swift academically. We were strongly attracted to each other. Dislike her and women? Afraid of her and women in general? Hear me: no way—not at all.

Even as a priest, I have been deeply attracted to many women. Sharing the priesthood of Christ did not and does not diminish my human nature. Put another way, being a priest does mean jettisoning my manhood. In Africa, there were many women with whom I was close. And indeed loved in the priestly and Jesus manner. This is celibate love. Some of them have died. All have aged. Some were nuns or single women or wonderful married women. All were my friends, none of whom I exploited but all of whom were dear friends. In the United States, I have met and admired and befriended scores of women. To this day we have loving friendship and (sorry to disappoint the street-smart guys) they consider me warm and loving and funny and great to be around.

And there are thousands like me—nuns and brothers and priests who understand experientially that love is a helluva lot more than sex alone. We do have our clinkers and maybe even the street-smart set has its own clinkers. Are the critics and the moderns all so perfectly balanced that they never go to shrinks or divorce lawyers or all-night bars where they can have access to sleeping pills?

As a practicing psychologist, I have been leading groups for years, groups mostly of young people with huge, crippling difficulties with interpersonal relationships. Most of the time the problems center around what look like sexual behavior but which, upon closer examination, turn out to be problems of self-esteem or self-concept. The oft repeated insistence on the correctness of sexual intimacies seems strangely linked to what appears to be a frantic attempt to justify such behavior. A young person will fiercely insist that all that is really needed is to accept the naturalness of sexual intimacy. Everyone is doing it. All we have to do is relax and accept our actions. We must throw off the inhibitions of the past and so on and so on.

I am startled and dismayed but even at times pleased. Why pleased? I am a Catholic priest. Why do they come to me to speak of actions clearly antithetical to the Catholic code? Do they expect and want some kind of punishment?

Do they know—on some deep unconscious level—that they are self-destructive and seek some kind of rescue from Father? Or Mother Church?

When I point out the inconsistency and incongruity of their life stance and when I ask: "If sexual behavior really frees you from emotional constriction, what are you doing here—in a shrink's office?" They boggle and stammer and close down. Really now, babe, who is the mixed up one?

I have been asked at least one hundred times: "Jimmy, didn't you ever want to get married?" To which I jauntily reply: "At least a thousand times." Of course, marriage is powerfully attractive. Of course, a loving sexual union with a beautiful wife is very alluring. Of course, having one's own children has incredible and profound appeal. But there is a very big something else. There is an overwhelming call from God which every consecrated celibate understands as so pre-articulate, so intense, so persistent that one simply chooses (note the word carefully) with freedom the beautiful and fulfilling love which is God Himself. This is a love which is so freeing that it allows the celibate one to love others non-possessively, purely and generously.

So, to the street-smart crowd. There is a view other than yours which pleases and fulfills many; a view which liberates and does not smother; a view which nurtures and fosters growth and which goes out to others away from narcissistic leanings. Try to understand. Be a little open minded or at least try to listen. Perhaps, you might get a glimmer of why this kind of love is real and why it makes, not schizoids but supple, attractive, enviable human beings. Hang out with a couple of them some time and try to shelve (even temporarily) any bias you might have about consecrated chastity. You might even want to try celibacy yourself. Gabrielle Brown Ph.D. did and she wrote a book about it: *The New Celibacy: Why More Men and Women Are Abstaining from Sex—And Enjoying It* (McGraw-Hill, 1980).[1]

Don't knock it. You may be talking about something someone loves.

Priests and Women—A Question!

When I was eight years old, I was convinced that Catholic priests and nuns did not walk like the rest of us. They floated. They glided. They had invisible celestial wings which flapped in a way known only to the great God. They were surely angelic and couldn't possibly belch, with satisfaction, after a delicious Italian meal, like the rest of us—to say nothing of more physical behaviors so common to mankind.

The infallibility of the religious sister was more than legendary. The ultimate silencer of all debate was simply, "Sister sez." Sister simply knew. That was all there was to it! When Sister spoke, God spoke. She couldn't possibly be wrong. Even though she spoke gently and quietly, her power was enormous—just because of who she was. And when Father spoke from the pulpit pounding the lectern with his godly fist, we listened in awe and just knew that this was the very word of the Lord Himself. We were delighted to see the great man get all worked up ordering us to follow the right and holy way.

Even up to my entrance into the seminary in my early twenties, I was still enthralled by a pedestal-perception of priests. It, however, had deepened my internal struggle when I decided to try my hand at priesthood. It was a struggle because priests, I thought, can't really like girls. And I do. But priests don't really need to like girls. How could they when they really don't have the same kind of emotional life and physical needs as the rest of us? In the fourth grade I was emotionally captured by Marie Becker, a skinny, dark-eyed girl who lived on 62nd street—far from my home zone of *sixty-foist* street. In high school, the pretty girls in saddle shoes and good bods who danced the Lindy Hop and talked so knowledgeably about Glen Miller and Benny Goodman utterly fascinated me.

When I became a freshman in college and tried to smoke a pipe in the then current cool climate, I dated the best-looking girl in the parish. How she could dance! She was really cool even if a bit slow academically—that didn't matter since she knew the latest steps and liked to smooch with me Then came these powerful scruples. Liking girls somehow didn't fit with what I was thinking of doing. However, I was encouraged when I heard the scuttlebutt in the seminary that after ordination somehow God fitted the priest with what the inner circle called "tin pants." No longer would the ordained cleric in the Catholic Church have to worry about sexual attractions toward the good-looking woman who wanted to discuss her spiritual life with the young priest (who looked so freshly scrubbed right out of the seminary box). He would have no need for or involvement with females beyond the strictest boundary of his pastoral obligation. He would need no input from the female world. He had it all. Any relationship beyond the immediately professional was not only unnecessary but probably highly suspect.

He would be the clerical parallel of Shane, the loner cowboy and gunslinger who comes into a tough town, cleans it up, straightens out a farm for a klutz, resists the obvious lure of the klutz's wife who sexually pants for him, even distances himself from an eleven-year-old boy who idolizes him and then rides off alone into the sunset for his next assignment. He needs no one. Everyone needs him. He is the complete Mr. Fixit whose strength comes from some source distinct from those whose lives he touches. He is a kind of Christ figure.

The collision of that somewhat romantic view of the priesthood hit me forcefully and immediately after the oils were placed on my New York hands. By God's grace and my own good sense from then till now after fifty-six years of exciting and satisfying ministry, I have balanced relatively successfully the aspects of my being an *alter Christus* with my emotional Gaelic/Hebraic personality. I have had many wonderful women friends who were neither mother nor sister nor aunt nor nanny for me. Nor were they lovers. They were in a special category which I shall attempt to describe, at least operationally. With that goal, I have looked with empathic affectivity on the following:

Fr. W. E., a giant of a priest, powerful leader of souls, a no-drink, no-smoke, no-swear, totally uncompromising celibate, had a long-term relationship (i.e., strictly non-genital) with a nun with whom he exchanged intimate soul secrets for years. He claimed that his masculinity was deepened by his intercourse[2] with this religious woman. In no way was his priesthood compromised nor was his mental life dominated by what the modern swain describes as "being crazy about her." Adding a fifth category to C.S. Lewis's *Four Loves*, I suggest Father E. and Sister M. had a great love for each other which operated satisfactorily for God's work from both their points of view, and for their own stability in their respective vocations.

Fr. J.M.G., brilliant, international orator, prolific author, will of steel, fearless in facing down any public figure on challenges to the Church, unquestioned integrity and chastity, had a companion, a Miss C., often at his side, his secretary and more. She was a woman of great character and ability who, beyond her professional value to Fr. G., was also a listening post off whom he could bounce his prodigious ideas. Their relationship was known to all and unquestioned by all and evidently mutually valuable.

Fr. J. McS., a veritable intellectual giant, historian/scholar, master spiritual director of women (married, single and vowed religious), prolific author. The essence of personal discipline. Known for his iron will. His constant companion whom he had baptized into the body of Christ, H. M., herself a scholar, would spend hours with him each evening, talking, praying, working on a new manuscript. She referred to him as Father, as if there simply were no other cleric in the world. Each night he would walk her to the corner on her way home, greet her goodnight with a courtly lifting of his hat. Apparently, even the giants can fit their needs for appropriate gender complementarity into the glorious structure of the priesthood!

Fr. J.M., a quiet industrious scholar who wrote the most successful catechism for enquirers up to his time. He was deep into the work of sharing faith with others and instructed and baptized literally hundreds of people into the Catholic Church. Among these was B., a professional woman, highly intelligent, an author who became devoted to Fr. M. even unto his final years when he regressed into a kind of mutism and childishness typical of some very aged persons. She tended him daily as companion, feeding him, walking him and seeing to his every need. What would one call this devotion? Is it some kind of love which is clearly real and obviously chaste? No eyebrow was raised in his circle. No speculation. No remarks. By some kind of intuition everyone, including me, was struck by what I am now categorizing as fifth love.

Fr JBS, author, attorney, credentialed to argue before the US Supreme Court. Editor of an outstanding Catholic intellectual magazine. Internationally respected ecumenist. V.K., an attractive, charming professional woman who had a warm, close but chaste relationship with Fr JBS which was known and supported by his colleagues, clerical and lay. In my assessment, it looks like classic C.S. Lewis.

I recall my own Aunt Maggie and her relationships with priests. Unmarried, highly educated with great skills, an Irish beauty anxious to help the Fathers with their sermons and manuscripts, she entertained them in our apartment many times as they obviously came only for spiritual or professional reasons. Fr. Bas, called by many of his contemporaries a saint (who used a hair shirt for penance reasons), would sit with her in the parlor holding her hand speaking of celestial things. We thought it beautiful. No one had any thought of the inappropriate.

The examples are multitudinous. Tell me about Francis and Clare. Or Francis de Sales and Sr. de Chantal. Teresa of Avila and John of the Cross. It all sounds so beautiful in the pious books. But is it really as it appears to be? Is this all merely fifth love? With reasonable cynicism, it seems to me (a crotchety old priest dinosaur) to be fatuous and naïve to believe that such idyllic relationships function every time a Catholic priest crosses the life path of a woman (especially should she be pretty and cute and slightly *chasseuse de soutane*). Our history is replete with the tragic behaviors of priest philanders and sexually-teasing women. To our regret the beauty of the Church has been soiled by those on both sides who have exploited the weaknesses and needs of others. Common sense and normal prudential judgment were cast aside, utterly disregarding the sage rule of Michaleen Flynn, the little marriage broker of *Quiet Man* fame, who insisted to his clients that the proprieties will be observed: "No patty fingers."

We have been told almost ad nauseam that priests are just like the rest of men—yet I have seen some priests who do seem Shane-like, needing little from others, completely dedicated giving the boot to the modern saw that men go nuts if they can't have sex. Statistically, most priests seem happy and contented; they like themselves, laugh a lot, are likeable and seem as normal as the average married man. In fact, the studies commissioned for such research show a far healthier group of professional men (priests) than the media happy presentations of ex-priest social scientists who still battle the guilt of their leaving the priesthood. In my extensive marital counseling practice and career I have seen firsthand the shallowness of the stance that all one needs is a sexual life to be happy. Some of the most certifiable clients I have treated have been males with active sexual experience. However, the quality of the Catholic priesthood (out of the ken of the secular researcher) is God's grace which sustains and makes possible the beauty known as celibate chastity. As Cardinal George of Chicago reminded us, to believe that chastity in itself is impossible is to disbelieve in the resurrection of Jesus. It is that fundamental.

Some priests are completely uninterested in a relationship with a woman—perhaps they are homosexual, latent or otherwise. Some have low libido. Some are so self-absorbed that a relationship with a woman would detract from their central focus—themselves! I recall being shocked as a newly ordained priest when a very old and super cynical priest informed me that a then very popular media priest was too egotistical to have woman trouble. I had no idea what he might have meant. Some priests carry early repressed memories of anti-women irritation, recalling their early family life when their female siblings hung their stockings and lingerie in the one shower used by the entire family.

There is a statistically negligible (but disastrous) percentage of sociopathic pervert priests who have deceived gullible and pressure-driven recruiters with high sounding politically correct phrases. These few are the classic Pavlovian/John Watson stimulus/response types who are drawn almost automatically to touch women inappropriately. These are the albatrosses who have dragged the goodness and holiness of Catholicism through the slime.

Such a run through of priest tendencies might be nothing more than a description of the male population in general. Yet, in the priest population there exists—at least ideally—a significant difference. This is in the reasonably expected total interior dedication of this man to his God. Such dedication is rightfully to be followed. The Catholic Church clearly has a right to this dedication.

Similarly and surely, the married man is reasonably expected to be interiorly dedicated to his wife alone. Adultery can occur in ways other than the physical. His wife, his family, society have a right for its own wellbeing to demand that fidelity. We recall, with clarity, the strong admonition of Jesus, radical for His time, that a man can sin even in thought by lusting in his heart for a woman other than his wife. Where are you, Jimmy Carter?

So as to the question which should be bluntly posed: is the priest to be completely isolated from women, their ideas, their suggestions, their friendship, their love, their very presence? Is he to be involved in study, prayer, reading, writing and contemplation only? Is the priest to be totally male oriented? Is he to view (even at the unconscious level) the female world as inimical to not only his priesthood, his sexuality, but also to the actual work he is called to do? Should he be emotionally locked in a symbolic ivory tower engrossed in some spiritual facsimile of books, animals or viruses?

Or is the priest to jettison this whole idea of being away from everyone? Does he now feel that he so needs women (like other men) that he can rightfully have a relationship (in modern context, this term implies genital behavior)? Is he now the regular guy, the big ha ha, who hangs out with the secular gang, drinking, smoking, telling the blue story, with a little occasional sex (or maybe a little grass)? Is he to ignore the possible unwise dedication of a single women who might pass up her own chances for marriage in her friendship with Father? Does he ignore possibilities of scandal?

Or is there some kind of fifth-love middle ground? This is risky territory which can be navigated only with ruthless honesty, deep personal prayer and courageous spiritual direction. The notion of complementarity does seem to have some healthy and spiritual dimension which same-sex relationships cannot. Are the real data in? We don't know but the question deserves to be asked and certainly must be answered. Perhaps, there is no general rule. Perhaps it is individual. Whatever it is, the holy and honest answer has to be in congruence with the teaching and experience of Christ's Church. Whenever there might be a doubt, the resolution always must be in favor of Jesus and His Magisterium. Let the debate begin!

A Woman as a Catholic Priest? A Suitable Subject at the Pope's Burial?

It has been estimated that over two billion people around the world watched some aspect of the wake and funeral of John Paul II ("JPII") who is already being called the Great. The vox populi (or voice of the people) for the first time in hundreds of years is chanting "*santo subito*" or "make him a saint now." Obviously, his incredible charisma and personal holiness captured much of the world. The airtime of television and radio and the space in the print media, focused, in a most unprecedented manner, on him and his unbelievable achievements over a twenty-six-year reign as Pope. The spotlight was on John Paul II. The understandable but out-of-place questions like, "Who will the next pope be?" "Will he depart from the position of JPII on women's ordination?" "Where will he stand on same-sex marriages?" All should be tabled until we have fully mourned and respected the man who possibly was the greatest Pope in a thousand years. Taste has a symmetry which should be observed.

Hence it seemed to many that the dragging in of negative comments about what he didn't do in his years as Pope, was the acme of poor taste and tackiness. We were all present in our own personal ways both to bury and praise JP II. It is not only a case of *nihil nisi bonum de mortuis* (don't speak ill of the dead). It is also an insensitivity to the feelings of millions of mourners who truly feel the profound sense of loss and who need space to grieve. It is no time to engage in grumpy polemics or the advocacy of one's own agenda.

Greatness of personal life and achievement does not mean the perfection which still belongs to God alone. Even the greatest person who ever lived would have some aspect of the not-done.

Shrill demonstrators advocating abortions rights or gay marriage or lay power grabs or attention for clerical molestation victims of thirty years ago have all surfaced this week and have generally been treated as mere publicity seekers. They were all seeking their own agenda with minimal focus on grief. However, one addendum to this sorry list which has received almost reverential attention has been the subject of women's ordination. The writer was invited the day of the Pope's funeral to participate in a panel on a major cable network which was supposedly to range over the Pope's life and work but which instead focused largely on the need to dialogue the subject of the woman as a Catholic priest. My poor health prevented me from the participation to my own great frustration. Given the tasteless direction the panel took, had I been there, I, with no future anywhere except heaven and with no need for approval from the female lobby, would have been driven myself to articulate a particular view.

Being the dinosaur that I am, I would have enjoyed the opportunity to tell the little joke of the 1995 era which reflected what most mainline theologians thought at that time.

The Pope sees the Lord in a dream Who grants him three questions that JP II might need to solve. JPII asks:

1. "Will there ever be married priests" The Lord replies: "Not in your lifetime."

2. "Will all religions unite under a common belief?" The Lord replies: "Not in your lifetime."

3. "Will there ever be women priests.?" The Lord replies: "Not in my lifetime."

I recall that in my television years at NBC, I interviewed a seething woman theologian, from St. John's University in 1960 on the subject of women's ordination. She confidently predicted that a woman would be ordained a priest possibly in 1985, or in 2010, with probability or in 2035, with certainty. Her predictions seem wan and anemic today particularly in the light of the stance of the Church through the articulation of Pope John Paul II, the Great. As General MacArthur proclaimed on the USS Missouri in Tokyo Bay in 1945: "This case is now closed." Also, Monsignor William Smith, the highly respected American theologian, opined after the Pope's death: "The Pope was not giving his personal opinion. He was simply voicing the official position of the Church." Apparently, some wistfully hope that the ban on ordination of women is simply the verbalization of a kind of Neanderthal, super-conservative Slav which will be nullified with the election of a more modern and progressive Pope. Yet John Paul II proclaimed not his personal opinion but the voice of the Holy Spirit speaking through the Magisterium.

Women cannot be ordained priests of the Catholic Church (cf. Pope John Paul II's letter *Ordinatio Sacerdotalis* of May 1994). Still, the drums beat and the demonstrations go on. And will continue to do so. This is more than theology. This is also a psychological question. When one meets a fully mature and educated woman like Sr. Sarah Butler, professor of Theology at the seminary of St. Joseph in Yonkers, New York, and an accredited theologian to the Vatican, one can listen with respect and full attention to her understanding of the point. She clearly points out why one must submit to the Church's stance which she explains is based on theology. For a full look at her careful reasoning, one might consult her article in the *Chicago Studies Theological Journal* of April 1995. In sum she asks three basic questions all of which are answered in the negative.

1. Does the Church teach the subordination of women?

2. Are women barred from full participation in the Church?

3. Is the ministerial priesthood the subject of a right?

Sr. Butler's great strengths lie not only in her superior scholarship but also in the profound understanding of the glories of her womanhood and her equal but different role in the great plan of salvation.

It is unseemly to argue that one's genitalia are the criterion of being a priest as so many of these howling advocates endlessly shout. There is a famous story in the annals of the New York Archdiocese priest lore which highlights this conjecture. Allegedly, a priest was giving the Last Rites or the Sacrament of the Anointing of the Sick, anointing the forehead of the dying person with his thumb when a modern-type nun, hospital chaplain, somewhat sarcastically remarked to him: "If I had a ______________ [male phallus] I could do that, too." He replied, "That's funny, I always use my finger."

Psychologists always look for hidden or unconscious meanings of words. Is there some kind of rejection of one's own femininity encased in these angers? When one meets the angry, screaming females with almost neutered male cohorts, one begins to intuit another dimension. Their allegation is one of sheer nobility stating that the only reason she wishes to be ordained is to care for Christ's faithful in the Eucharist. Eucharistic availability is surely a legitimate reason for seeking more vocations to the priesthood. But there may be other motivations unknown to her conscious life. Does she want to be a man? If even unconsciously? Is she bent on psychically castrating her own father by bringing down Father to her level or raising herself to his? Is she feeling oppressed by men with a need to retaliate? Does she see that she is, in effect, seeking and reverting back to an elitism or clericalism which has been the bane of the clergy for centuries?

One of my religious brother priests, a certified archivist, was present at an ecumenical meeting of archivists at a renowned Episcopal church in New York City. The Rector was introducing the first woman priest of that church. The new "priest" was built like a linebacker, in black skirt, brown tweed jacket and Anglican style clerical collar. She approached my colleague who is small in stature and thrust out a beefy hand and said in a deep voice: "Hi, I'm Father Ralph." My colleague swears and avers to the truth of this incident.

Perhaps, more time should be spent in broadening people's minds with the glorious intellectual and aesthetic tradition of our Church rather than hurling raging remarks around the world and seeking androgynous couture.

Following Sister Butler's insights, I suggest that the plaintive cry for full participation really points up two needs: first, the need to promote and support more effectively the vocation and mission of all the baptized. Not just in direct and ecclesial service but in the real marketplace. And second, the need to find adequate ways, formal and informal, to incorporate the true, many and wonderful gifts of women into the public life of the Church. Anything else is blowing a lot of futile and angry hot air into what could be a loving and exciting modern Church. Or as some fancy writers put it: "It's time to stash the balderdash."

Why Self Pity Can Kill You!

I was introduced to the world of psychiatry, psychology and mental illness by Dr. Rudolph Allers, an Austrian psychiatrist, who had been a disciple of Dr. Sigmund Freud, and under whom he became disillusioned, subsequently writing his own monumental work, *The Successful Error* (Cluny Media, October 21, 2019). He, after the fashion of many heavy hitter thinkers of that era, ultimately became a Catholic, going on to become professor of psychiatry at the Catholic University, Washington, D.C. His classes were packed to the doors not with weirdoes of shrinkery but with intellectually hungry students of religion seeking some understanding of *gratia supponit naturam* (grace builds on nature).

Stereotypic to the extreme, he had shaggy, long gray hair, wore thick glasses on the end of his long nose which fairly shrieked of his Eastern European heritage. He delighted us with quaint 19th-century courtly prose, his Germanic accent charmingly right out of the Madame Du Barry-like salons of elegant Vienna. His sentence construction was original and humorous. We roared with laughter. for example, when he described the talkativeness of the elderly as "excessive activity of the articulatory organs."

During his year of lectures, always without notes, and delivered looking up at the classroom ceiling, he took us through symptoms and treatment of the various neuroses and psychoses which we dutifully scribbled into our notebooks. We went through endless mental mechanisms of defense, and the many interfaces of religion and psychiatry. It was all terribly fascinating yet most of our notes were deposited into that great educational dustbin so dear to all graduate students once the final exams were over.

Apart from the indelible impression he made upon me that science and religion, properly understood, made congenial bedfellows, I remember very little, if anything, of his content. Except for one powerful point. He devoted one lecture to a startling statement. "Self-pity is the most damaging of all the human emotions." It was a daring and bold absolutist position. Clearly as a graduate student, I didn't have the foggiest as to the depth of his meaning. But my own years as therapist, counselor and spiritual director have opened some of his wisdom to me. How many times I have been frustrated by the endless self-defeating behavior of so many of my clients (patients or directees) as they exemplified over and over again the old axiom, "I am my own worst enemy."

To walk with someone through the dark valley of depression and self-fulfilling prophecy, while a sacred privilege, is a most heavy and sometimes discouraging task.

I recall a forty-three-year-old nurse whom I was supervising in her clinical work, pursuant to her gaining a graduate degree in Counseling. When she was thirteen years of age, she was (she claimed) sexually abused by a family member. Obviously, the profound scarring, confusion, anger, and disorientation of such a tragic experience are not easy to overcome. My work with sexual abuse victims has clearly illustrated the hurt and the insecurity associated with such ugly victimization. This is especially true if the victim is a child or adolescent. Even adults have enormous difficulty managing such horrendous insult to their psyche. Yet, one must heal, or one must face the prospect of "half" living. I recall the comical presentation in Hollywood's *Analyze This* (1999) in which the psychiatrist. while continuing the soothing external protocols with the patient, internally says to the whining woman, "Why the [expletive deleted] don't you get yourself a life?"

How often therapists react in this manner knowing full well, even with their own irritation, that the patient is killing himself emotionally and blocking any kind of satisfying life with God, neighbor or self. He is doing this to himself! What price must we pay to be free of this paralyzing pattern? What does it take to give up the clinging to wrongs, real or perceived, which interfere with one's sense of well-being?

The nurse (my supervisee) was having difficulty in her field work in a certified clinic. Instead of focusing on her own patient, she invariably brought the work to focusing on herself and her personal problems, mainly her recollection of incest. She seemed, almost, to seek sympathy from her own patients. She constantly spoke to them of her abuse, alleging to herself that this was a form of identifying with the patient. However, she had problems keeping clients who constantly failed to keep appointments and communicated simultaneously various non-verbal messages of discontent. Though reasonably intelligent, she was plain looking with a rather flat personality, making her just another bland face in the crowd. Her one claim to fame was her victimization.

In the group experience required of our interns, she would constantly refer to her abuse thirty years earlier, time after time. Apart from this, her specialty, she had little to say. When I pointed this out to her as a facet of her training deficiency, she became furious with me that I did not understand, that men can't possibly empathize with a woman in such a situation and similar old saws. Some of it might have been true but her fixation, nonetheless, was stultifying her ability in the helping profession as well as hurting her chances for personal happiness. One factor we all saw was that should she give up her tiresome and repetitious verbalization of the old wound, she would have nothing to offer since all her intervening years had focused on refining and honing this single event. If I give this up, I can never get the limelight. I will be a wallflower. But were not there any other and positive dimensions to her life? Did she not, like all human beings, have a glass that was either half filled or half empty? The self-pity would blind her to her other positive dimensions which might be a source of satisfaction for her.

Her life had been focused on "poor me." There was legitimacy to her anger and sadness but there was also an emotional imbalance which did not serve her well. This is the self-pity described by Dr. Allers or the pity pot so popular with twelve-step programs. It did not help her one iota but became, instead, a bitter, raging, self-absorbed way of life. It was pernicious to her happiness as Allers had predicted. So, is there a way of getting over it? Can a person learn to let go?

I have been struck by the pervasive nature of the self-pitying phenomenon in several of my patients who have been savagely abused by Church employees, (priests, deacons, teachers, janitors and even nuns). All of them have been severely damaged and certainly deserve full attention vis-à-vis their healing. Those who don't heal, by some strange inner incapacity, seem almost to refuse to improve. This is puzzling until the pity pot raises its ugly head.

That the molestation might have occurred twenty or thirty years ago, that the molesters are dead, senile, in nursing homes or prison, expelled in disgrace, that many of my patients have received substantial sums of money, is all irrelevant. There is some kind of narcissism, some kind of semi-pleasurable navel gazing involved in the near stubborn clinging to my story. Is there an insatiable need to tell the horror to anyone who will listen? Why do my patients call me on the telephone, day or night, demanding an immediate ear to rail over and over again at that so-and-so? The waste of time and energy given over to retelling a thousand time told tale is staggering.

There is probably a linkup or correlation between this patently irrational (can I say dumb?) behavior and self-esteem. I note that patients who have a strong ego system seem to do much better. They seem able to cast off the unpleasant or terrifying experience and ultimately get on with lives of enjoyment and productivity, even relegating the molester to the category of nut or psycho. They report definite feelings of anger, confusion, disorientation, betrayal or even just irritation but refuse to give undue attention to this episode. There is a sense that focusing too heavily on these episodes only fuels that inner turmoil and makes healing that much slower. (In cases of repeated molestation, there is an entirely different affective reaction which might involve some consent from the victim, especially in ephebophilic situations.)

In a meeting of several Catholic professional psychologists, the group was asked whether a single grab of the bottom would wreak long term emotional havoc with a victim. This was probing the psychological effect on the victim. Consensually, the response was a definite no, particularly if the victim was reasonably healthy and if there was opportunity to discuss the event with a trusted other. In the cases of the brutal and exploitative repeated behavior which we have studied, the consequences are obviously different. Yet, even in those cases, after a reasonable airing and analysis, it is clinically and spiritually better for the victim to begin to focus on the positive side of his life in general and to glimpse what is meant by moving on. To remain stuck on an insatiable plane of poor me means misery and bitterness. When my patients tell me that they simply can't stop their obsessive mental behavior (and this is behavior), I will challenge them with all kinds of specifics which are available to them for happier living. And often with concrete improvement.

These specifics are useable not only for the disastrous type tragedies mentioned above but are also helpful for lesser, but nonetheless crippling, personality formations tempting most human beings. The bug of poor me, I suspect, hampers all of us in differing degrees. What does the normal human being do to cope with the temptation to sit on that pity pot? Get a sense of humor implant? Hardly! (Even though there is little to compare with the healing ability of laughter.)

Why not use the faith? The Catholic faith is pragmatic, if anything, which, in this instance, means that the faith does show how to deal with this killing self-pity. The faith almost screams out the notion of living one day at a time. The twelve-step programs heavily depend on this specific. The past is gone. The unknown future is not here. Only now is here—wherein we live and move and have our being. The great St. Teresa of Avila wrote of her living not one day at a time but living one minute at a time. Anything more for her was intolerable. The faith teaches that the good Lord gives only those crosses which one can handle. (How I used that when I struggled against my crippling claustrophobia in the MRI tube). As my old grandmother taught me: "Jamie, God fits the back to the burden." The birds of the air and the lilies of the field are nothing in God's sight compared to His love for any human being. His powerful grace is right there waiting to be used! With His help, I can handle anything He allows. What blocks our using the help of God? Maybe, I don't ask for it!

And what about the famous half-filled/half-empty approach?

An old timer like me knows very well the inevitable pains, inconveniences and indignities associated with old age. I know the loneliness of being a dinosaur. I know what it feels like to be passed over. I am aware of my own failures over the years. My past poor judgments are ever with me in bright colors and sharp density. As a retiree from a previous post of influence and clout, I know what it feels like now to be just another face in the crowd. This is viewing the glass as half empty.

However, seeing the half-filled glass has me exuberant that I have been sustained by what P.D. James, the aging English mystery writer, calls "the magnificent irrationality of faith."

I made my First Holy Communion when I was seven years old and was euphoric that I received my Lord and my God in the Eucharist. I have never lost that euphoria into my 84th year. I have been blessed beyond calculation coming from a loving, wild and somewhat crazy family which have given me the enormous and profound certainty of my own lovability. I have had beautiful friends whom I have loved and who have loved me. I have seen the glory of God's world festooned by man's gifts. I have been blessed to study at many universities. I have been blessed to have shared the life journey of hundreds of fellow children of God as I practice my art of psychotherapy and spiritual direction. Is there space enough in the world for me to record my blessings?

The cells of my old body have renewed themselves many times, I know, since that seven-year-old kid met Jesus in the Eucharist. If I am cell-wise different I can still recognize that urchin from the Westside in my deeper self. I am fairly much the same. But have I grown? Oh, yes! I am different and the same, simultaneously, so grateful for what I have had and have—and still having so much fun—even with the creaking bones and the not-too-far-away death!

Does self-pity fit in here? I do my best to keep it far away because it kills. I love life and wish to enjoy what is left for me. I make my thanks to the Good Lord and His loving holy Mother who smiles at me so often, encouraging me to gratitude rather than to self-pity.

Is Devotion to the Mother of God Antediluvian?

Dr. Paul Chaim Scheneck, a Jewish intellectual who converted to Catholicism, once noted, in discussing his conversion, that sometimes the heart does not understand or accept what the mind can know. All the logic, the data, the experience are irrelevant when the heart is closed. No matter what is presented, the response is negative. Nothing can persuade because from the beginning the heart has said that it is not possible. "I will not agree." Dr. Scheneck had all the logic and the proof needed but it was not enough. It simply couldn't be. It recalls for me the famous remark in a religious debate which stunned us all. "Don't confuse me with the facts." Such a position annihilates any exploration as to a possible other side.

But isn't the opposite likewise compelling? If one's heart embraces and is supported by a dimension unavailable to immediate intellectual verification, it is very difficult to move through pre-judgment to a supple and rich emotional or spiritual life. The juvenile demand for empirical proof can be utterly deadly to growth and warmth. The skeptic will demand proof of love and honor and patriotism and appreciation, draining life of its possibilities of profound joy. "I feel it but I don't believe it" is compared with the other mode, "I see it with my mind's eye but I can't accept it." That can be the end of any significant exploration.

Let me explore a concrete instance. The practice of an unquestioning and loving devotion to Mary, the Mother of Jesus (Who, I believe, to be the Divine, Itself, in human nature) seems to be completely incomprehensible to many moderns. For example, a brilliant and devout Jewish woman who likes and respects me, cannot do other than characterize my Marian practice as antediluvian, i.e., prior to the flood which made Noah so famous. Perhaps, the given (for Catholics) of Christ's Divinity is so great a block for devout Judaism that any further probing is exceedingly difficult or impossible. Perhaps, for childlike Catholics like me (hopefully not childish) the warmth, comfort and "rightness" of such spiritual dynamics stem not from heavy intellectual exegesis and theological rigor but from something else. Something terribly human (which yet smacks of the divine), which meets and fulfills my need to flesh out my own developing spiritual life. And that something, I sense, emanates from God which empowers me with an ability to see and humility to accept. Perhaps I probe for the affective as compared with the cognitive. Or is this the mysterious entity called grace?

When I was a child, I knew nothing of the glorious Cathedrals dedicated to Our Blessed Mother. I never heard of Chartres or Notre Dame, Ile de la Cite de Paris. I never knew of the towering music of Mozart and Schubert and Gregorian chant which incarnated the love of the BVM (Blessed Virgin Mary) into sensible, exalted forms. I never heard of the *Alma Redemptoris Mater* or the *Salve Regina* or the *Tota Pulchra Est, Maria.* I never heard of Wordsworth's famous line, "Our tainted nature's solitary boast" which he, the Protestant, applied to Mary, this Mother of the Lord. I never saw the magnificent statuary in the Metropolitan Museum of Art concretizing the Catholic love of Mary. I never heard of the *Pieta* of Michelangelo depicting the beauty of the Mother of God.

Whatever I learned about devotion to Mary, I received from my Irish Grandmother whose formal education ended with the third grade. She taught me, for example, that when I die, should they not allow me to enter by the front gates of heaven I should go around to the back and Our Lady, the Blessed Mother will let me in. This is because she has great love for me and will help me always. Grandmother told me that

Jesus set this up when he was dying a terribly painful death on a great cross. Just before He died, He made me and everyone else to be her children and she would always be there for me. She would always love me—no matter what! And I should love her back! And incidentally I note that Mel Gibson in his powerful movie, *The Passion of the Christ* (2004), presents Peter, agonized and distraught after his cowardly denial of the Lord, kneeling before Mother Mary, with great heartbroken tears rolling down his cheeks. She does not scold nor reject. She silently places her healing hand upon his head. "It is all right," she seems to be saying. "It is all right, my child." No matter what our sin is, Mary, our Mother, still loves us. This, it seems to me, is really affective.

Such childlike devotion has been of enormous help to me in my life—particularly in times of smashing life difficulties. I did not develop this view from the many formal impediments I have met, such as ponderous professors who took themselves very seriously and who insisted that I plow through boring and sterile tomes written by academics who lived in metaphorical and real ivory towers.

I was amazed how quickly I was able to jettison the cumbersome balderdash backpack of academe. How quickly and gratefully I reverted back to the joy of my youth as I continuously recited and applied the first prayer I ever learned: "Pray for us now and at the hour of our death." For example, I recall being on a slow moving, coal burning night train, trudging across the Great Karoo of South Africa. The windows wouldn't close. The lights wouldn't work. The soot poured in through the open windows. I felt lonely and dirty and afraid. So, I did my beads, i.e., my Rosary, and prayed as I envisioned the mysteries of Christ's life, which were the main events of His death and redemptive sacrifice. I saw her there, He and my Mother, sharing His pain and His meaning. As the beads passed through my fingers I felt release, both emotional and physical and found, even with tears streaming down my cheeks, a calm and peace entering my being. This is not the security blanket of the *Peanuts* comic strip. This is the presence of my heavenly Mother who has always been there for me at critical times.

How many millions of Catholics over the years have had the same experience? Yet there have been all kinds of clever or cute attempts to make nice with devotion to the BVM. In order to counter any latent uncomfortable feelings that devotion to her is somehow detracting from devotion to Him, who is all and above all, some skittish Catholics have come up with fanciful stories and devices to counteract the harmful antics of big mouths like me. However, some do have some credence and possible utility. I recall the little thing about the schoolboy rebutting the scoffing college professor who claimed that there is no difference between His (Jesus') mother and my mother. The kid jauntily replies: "Yeah, but there is a big difference between the sons." Touché! And okay but it doesn't really move me.

Or the little kid, with his prayer for a bicycle unanswered, yelling at the statue of Jesus, "I'm gonna tell your mother!" The implication is clearly that the Mother of the Lord has great influence with the Divine One and will properly castigate the unresponsive Jesus. The kid extrapolates from his experience with his own mother and applies it directly to the Blessed Mother. Again, okay. While coming close to affectivity, this doesn't really move me either, even though I can understand because of my relationship with my own earthly mother.

Or astronomical metaphors like He, being the sun, and she, being the moon, who shines only by reflection from Him— very true and very intellectual but not sufficiently affective for me. Since each of us, like David fighting Goliath, with a mere sling shot and some stones rather than with the fancy armor of

Saul, must choose our own weapons in this struggle called life, I choose the notion of a celestial mother loving me with a profound and pervasive love. And I find that love in my prayer: "Now and at the hour of my death."

The now of this prayer is enormously important to me. I personally focus my spiritual life on the great now. Spirituality to me must be pragmatic and helpful. For me, the academic tends more to irritate than to inspire. All my life I have been able to intuit or pre-articulately depend on the Blessed Mother for her immediate and ever-present assistance. Since, similarly, I am deep into the existential indwelling of the Holy Spirit and the presence of the Lord, this approach—devotion to the loving Blessed Mother—is exceedingly meaningful to me. Yesterday or tomorrow, certainly, has some effect on my life but the dominant dimension is now—which I find each time I say to her: "Pray for us (me) now."

In particular, I find her gentle urgings in my heart when I suffer difficulty being obedient to the Lord's will—when I want my own way in everything I do. I hear her exhortation from the wedding feast at Cana: "Do whatever He tells you." Since I am positive about her love for me and her wish for my happiness, when she tells me that His will is for my wellbeing, even if I don't understand or if I am tempted to struggle in defiance, I am drawn to do His holy will. She will never mislead me because she loves me.

When I boggle in my occasional dark night, and my trust in God tends to waver, there she comes again. I see her as she responds to Gabriel with his apparently ridiculous message: "Behold the handmaid of the Lord. Be it done to me according to His word." My lesson: I don't know how I will do it (whatever it is), but I will and can, if I trust in His word and His power as did my Blessed Mother.

When I have difficulty with my emotional balance, I listen to her Magnificat when she proclaims the astounding insight about humility: "Generations will call me blessed." She acknowledges and lives the truth of her life. There is no phony modesty here. There is the calm and clear statement of who she is. I learn from her that I do not deny my gifts and talents, nor do I deny my limitations. All is from God to be used for His glory and will. I cannot cavil and waste energy with spurious self-deprecation.

When I feel the turbulent scream of libido, I call upon her to help me maintain my sexual integration and respect for the great God-gift of sexuality. The Queen of Chastity is powerful!

As for the future—particularly my own death, I sense her presence also there for me—as she was for Joseph, her husband, as he left this life for heaven. She was there helping him, as she will—me! She died herself showing me the way. Though I am naturally fearful of death, terror has no priority. She will there for me leading me to her divine Son and eternal joy—again because of her love for me, personally!

Devotion to Mary antediluvian? Certainly for me it is not. After all I am one of those dinosaurs who believe in personal survival after death. So, on the contrary, it is most appropriate for this eight-four-year-old kid [one-hundred-and-one-year-old kid]. I believe in eternal life. My summation is in an old poem I recall only partially:

> If Christ should come on earth some summer's day
> And walk unknown upon our busy street
> I wonder how 'twould be
> If we should meet—
> And being God if He would act that way?
> Perhaps the kindest thing that He could do

Would be just to forget that I failed to pray
And clasp my hand forgivingly and say,
"My Child, I've heard my Mother speak of you."

To Speak or Not to Speak. Is Silence Always Golden?

Dante of *Divine Comedy* fame wrote: "The hottest places in hell are reserved for those who, in time of great moral crisis, maintain their neutrality."

Edmund Burke, the noted British Parliamentarian, wrote: "The easiest way for evil to succeed is for good men to do nothing." (Or say nothing?)

Elie Wiesel, the Jewish teller of tales and concentration camp survivor, wrote: "Silence in the face of oppression helps only the oppressor."

Jesus, the Lord and master of all, sternly reminds us that the lukewarm are nauseous to Him—a clear implication that serious Christians must take a position on crucial moral problems. Pope Benedict XVI wrote in 1985 with great lament about those Catholic leaders who teach with "studied ambiguity" when presenting the basic teachings of Catholicism. I am uncomfortably reminded of Yale's Stephen Carter with his definition of integrity: the person of integrity must be willing, if necessary, to verbalize his values regardless of consequences. What kind of Christian and masculine responsibility falls on me or on anyone else who seeks God's approval and one's own self-respect when we speak of clarity of personal stance?

Yet, in Ecclesiastes 3:7, we are told that there is "a time to be silent and a time to speak." Even the great and brave Thomas More, confronted by legally astute accusers seeking his very life for his refusal to endorse his king's unruly libidinous behaviors, faltered and hedged and ducked their attacks. He tried, in his own skillful and juridically experienced manner, every way to protect his life—principally by appealing to the age-old legal axiom: *Tacet, consensit!* Freely translated, this means: "By silence, one gives consent." Of course, ultimately, he was forced to verbalize his position and to face the brutal consequence of openness—his own decapitation. Sometimes, even saints waffle when facing fearsome possibilities. Nevertheless we, generally, do interpret one's silence on a serious issue to be an agreement with the stated proposition at hand.

Perhaps sometimes silence is golden. Perhaps it is prudent and helpful to be quiet in a specific circumstance. But sometimes silence is cowardice. Most of us have seen and sometimes even experienced the self-condemnation and dislike which comes with being cowed. I know that I should speak, but I do not. Why do I not—even when my own inner cowardice or inertia sickens me, psychically and morally?

Legitimate silence aside, why do we fear to speak up or disagree or confront? What are we really afraid of? How can one possibly understand the wimp reaction? Is it that one fears rejection of others? Does one have unresolved Oedipal conflict whereby he still unconsciously fears retaliation from his parent? Is it that I am never allowed to disagree? Is it all right to be disapproved? Must I always say yes to another's opinion and viewpoint? Is it all right to be the odd man out? Must everyone like me? Do I not have a right, as a child of the good God, to think my own thoughts and reach my own conclusions and live by them as I see fit?

The questions are rhetorical and the answers obvious. Yet for many of us it is a difficulty to speak up when facing evil or wrong or power even though we can get nauseated and revolted with sycophantic, bootlicking yes men who seek career advancement or temporary lollipops from those deemed powerful and bountiful.

Is it the profound fear of exclusion and social shunning which terrorizes me? I recall the once popular little book—*Jonathon Livingston Seagull* (by Richard Bach)—which details the inner life of a rebellious bird who pulls off from the herd because he cannot fly with the others in their manner. He seeks his own way, suffers the loss of his past and pursues what for him is authentic. Applied to human experience this can happen only if the person truly believes in his own values and convictions. Hence, Stephen Carter's suggestion that firstly one must know clearly what is authentic and real for him. Secondly, one must live in accord with the inner convictions and lastly one must be integral enough to verbalize such values.

I recall a specific example from my years in South Africa under the iniquitous social system called Apartheid. Helen Sussman, a white member of the Parliament, represented the non-European population of the country (i.e., anyone who was not white). While I basically disagreed with her communistic tinge, I admired her fearless insistence on the right to disagree with the overwhelming majority of politicians with whom she served. She was derided, shunned, isolated and mocked. Never did she falter. It was her own honest view which she persistently articulated as the political voice of the disenfranchised. Whether she was politically right or wrong is incidental to this paper. It is her integrity which is at issue.

Integrity has to insist that sometimes there are not two sides to an issue. The grisly Nazi Shoah has one side—an evil one. The rationalization and justification that Germany needed a pure race is inherently evil and wrong. Fancy talk cannot cover the core rot of this plan. Slavery is always wrong, regardless of the urgent pleas of a growing economy of the South. No one can own someone else. Only God owns us.

Same-sex marriage, similarly, is evil since it covers over inherently sinful behavior with the ambiguous plea for the right to love and for tolerance. The argument that NAMBLA[3], a movement to legitimize sexual relations between adult men and little boys, is inherently evil because it would destroy children almost beyond repair. When a couple perform pseudo sexual copulation in the vestibule of St. Patrick's Cathedral with the justification that the First Amendment protects their demonstration, there is no other side. Such behavior, besides being lewd and offensive *in se*, is also inherently evil.

The contention of this paper is simply this—integrity shrieks that such patent evil be called by its name. Euphemisms must be exposed as masks covering over what really is. To be silent lest one become unpopular is base. Whether or not Pope Pius XII in his alleged silence in World War II was strategically wise is strongly debated. Perhaps his silence helped save many lives but today it would appear that speaking the speech plainly is appropriate. Studied ambiguity should be avoided.

The world is filled with and knee deep with the people-pleasing population. We see all around us, amid the oases of healthy and self-respecting people, the hypocrite who says what he does not believe or denies what he does believe. A prime example is the with-it Catholic who, needing acceptance by the right people, wishes to appear sophisticated to the Georgetown/UN crowd and who joins in the chorus of criticisms and putdowns of the Church, who sneers at the notion that abortion is evil, exalts the right of homosexuals to marry and enthusiastically endorses moral relativism and who loudly proclaims to all that he is a Catholic and was once an altar boy, and perhaps even thought of entering the seminary. In fact, he is, as was stated in a recent *New Yorker* article, gradually becoming a non-Catholic who happens to go to Mass.

Actually, the person so described is a hypocrite. If he is that faithful Catholic he describes, he has the obligation (as pointed out by Archbishop Chaput of Denver in the May 2005 issue of the *Catholic Eye*) to speak the truth of soul if he is asked. If his criticisms and disagreements with basic Catholic teaching are what he really believes then, he should resign from the Church instead of pretending to be the devout believer. In either case, he is behaving with deceit. Nor can his behavior be called legitimate dissent (which is appropriate and necessary) since he departs from what is essential to the Catholic position where dissent is inappropriate. These Catholics, of course, might follow an honored family tradition of public worship. Let us pray that there is a sincere spiritual motivation impelling them. Keeping a nice public persona, carrying Bibles exiting churches on Sunday mornings might even have a bump upwards in the polls. Particularly if media people are present. Nevertheless, by their silence they show, at least, a disloyalty and, perhaps, a disbelief in basic Catholic teaching. Helen Sussman was not a hypocrite even if off course on spiritual matters.

These Catholics are, in the street term, phonies and from my point of view sadly lacking in integrity.

Jesus teaches that he who publicly acknowledges Him before the world will be acknowledged before the Father in Heaven. And, conversely and even frighteningly, those who deny Him before the world will be denied before the Father. But would I be shouting at the wind if I verbalize my own true convictions? Does it matter to anyone? Does it help anything? What do I gain other than derision and unpopularity?

In a large meeting of Catholic religious personnel held in New Mexico, convening the day after the November 2004 presidential election, the first two speakers publicly expressed their depression at the outcome and deeply lamented the behavior of those Catholic Bishops who dared to try to influence the Catholic vote. They wished that our leaders had kept silent and not made their own values known. Many heads nodded in vigorous agreement.

This writer, as the third speaker, to the contrary, expressed his own euphoria at the outcome, announcing that he had made a novena ending the day before the actual election aimed at the victory of the right candidate. His euphoria included the defeat of a so-called Catholic Senator, the Democratic leader, who had directed legislation uncongenial to Catholic convictions and values. Further, he applauded the bravery and the leadership of those Catholic Bishops who had the moral courage to clarify and publish the guidelines for a true Catholic conscience.

Many of these Catholic leaders (mostly self-described as liberal or progressive) looked at me aghast, mouths agape, wide-eyed, unbelieving. My expressed views were foreign to their taste and certainly I was considered Neanderthal. But apart from the complex causation of such widely different world views, can we assess the effect of such openness in a public forum? There is very little, if any, change in the thinking of others. The real value is within oneself, in the very soul of the one who dares to exercise integrity. Was it not the bard of Avon who urged: "This above all: to thine own self be true"? It is in the court of one's own soul that the meaningful judgment is given. I must face myself ultimately since I can run from me only so long. Yet, obviously, in the final analysis, only God's view of us is what really matters.

So now I ask myself what can they do to any of us, if we preface our view with the honest prefix, "from my point of view" or "it seems to me" or "it strikes me this way"? Can't one learn to disagree without being disagreeable? Perhaps, recourse to the Holy Spirit is the one practical way to handle this very human dilemma. When to speak and when to be silent. It can be a puzzlement. Let us pray for such light and courage.

Without it, we probably would profoundly dislike ourselves. In which case one might ask: "Is life worth living?" Heaven forbid. Does God make junk? Life is meant to be enjoyed. So, loosen my tongue, O Lord, and give me the courage to speak Your truth with humility, openness and compassion. Take from me fear and brutality. Help me to see that I can be wrong but also that I can be right and with Your help, my brave, if frightened, speech will not only help me but hopefully others of Your children.

Will the Real Catholic Church Please Stand Up!

The June 27, 2005 issue of *The New Yorker* carried a series of letters from a group of self-styled Catholics generally denigrating Pope Benedict XVI in response to a lengthy article by Peter J. Boyer entitled, "A Hard Faith." Interestingly, there were no letters counseling patience, no wait-and-see letters, no recognition of the towering intellect of the Pope and his quiet, sincere devotion to the Church over many years. This hard veering to the theological left by extreme dissidents illustrates and explains, in part, the current confusion about some basic questions: "What is the Catholic Church about anyway?" Or "What is the real Catholic teaching?" Or "Who is the Church?"

For example, one of the contributors was a nun of the modern variety who was aghast that some young seminarians would find her placard (which read Nuns for Kerry) scandalous. These young men were not tired old carryovers from the Woodstock era but bright and informed contemporary thinkers. That young Catholics would be upset by a nun supporting an extremely liberal Catholic who voted for abortion rights, same-sex marriage, late-term abortion and who claimed that his conscience was formed by Pope John XXIII, is apparently incomprehensible to her. How explain her unawareness of this existential contradiction? Or is it that she is irritated that today's young people are not buying into her patently obsolete and oxymoronic perception? Is it that Sister can't understand why young people don't see her view of the Church? Perhaps, she might recall that the magnetic and instant bonding between Pope John Paul II and young people was partially because he knew where they were spiritually and emotionally.

The same magazine in an editorial (May 2, 2005) innocently comments that certain matters do not concern faith like sexuality, celibacy, choice (presumably about abortion), the use of condoms, and stem-cell research (again presumably embryonic since the Church clearly supports appropriate stem-cell research). Such commentators would reduce the Church to the levels of irrelevance which characterize so many of the main-line Christian groups today. They urge us to be like so many others and endorse abortion and same-sex marriage. Teach pretty Bible stories, give to AIDS research and be nice and don't dig too deep. Demonstrate for the protection of whales and oppose oil exploration. But do stay on the sidelines of life. In effect these modern thinkers tell the Church what she ought to do and what to teach and how to behave for acceptance into the politically correct world. Or, more bluntly, become religiously castrated!

We saw a certain anguish at the election of a believing and courageous Pope when the modern Catholic had hoped for someone who would go with the times. Going with the times usually means unimpeded license to implement the politically correct list in the May 2nd comment noted above.

One such disappointed Catholic, on April 19, 2005, shouted, in St. Peter's Square, "He is the worst possible choice." Whom are we to believe? Who can tell us what is the Catholic Church's true position on life and eternity? Consider even the role of God Himself in our way of life and our political decisions. Is it healthy to have the Lord in the midst of everything? Is a public square unhealthy and unnatural where religious faith seems unwelcome and dangerous? Does the Catholic Church acquiesce to a public square stripped of God and religious faith? Incidentally, we might remember that the statement "Jesus is Lord" is not religious but political. Jesus was hung on a cross for His claim of Lordship. Christianity was illegal for the first 250 years of the Church's life because

Christians proclaimed in the public square (where the Emperor was all) that "Jesus is Lord" not Caesar. It looks to me to be a fairly obvious political focus.

So then, to whom does one go for the real Catholicism? Is there any real structure of orthodox Catholicism? There are so many voices claiming to have the authentic Catholic answer. Is it Catholics for a Free Choice which demands that abortion be removed from the categories of evil? They call themselves Catholic. Is it Richard McBrien? Or Charles Curran? Or Gregory Baum? They claim that they, as theologians, though controversial or dissident, are truly Catholic. Is the theologian more precisely Catholic than Pope Benedict XVI? Or is it that everyone is right and no one has a monopoly on denotative Catholic truth? Didn't someone note that "tolerance is the last virtue of a degenerate society"? Is Catholic truth to be operationally defined by well-heeled Catholics who, without knowing it, have gradually become non-Catholics and who happen to go to Mass for some anachronistic social or political reason? Does political and financial clout empower the big names to make theological decisions over the faith of the poor, little non-Harvard guy who just about makes it in life?

My old Irish Grandmother who went to the third grade in a parochial school knew the answer with ease. Jesus is the teacher. In the words of Bob Dylan, "Let us not talk falsely now, the hour is getting late." Catholicism obviously bases everything on the total belief in and trust of a loving God Who became man and died for our sins and by His resurrection promised us eternal life with Him. This divine Jesus left His legacy in a Church which He promised would never fail nor (in the ancient formulary) be overcome by "the gates of hell." This Church would be harassed and persecuted through the ages by Arians, Gnostics, Cathari, Albigensians, Jansenists, angry dissidents and slick talkers but would always survive, even if bloodied and weakened.

The Church would be burdened from the start with the Judas-type adherent, through hypocritical teachers and evil homosexual priest molesters of young people but would survive. It would produce thousands and thousands of holy women and men whom we call saints, publicly acclaimed or otherwise. It would be entrusted to Peter (Cephas) and his successors whom we have called Popes. These Popes in collegiality with those who succeeded the Apostles (Bishops) would articulate the teachings of Christ's Church with protection from the Holy Spirit of God Himself, and though they, themselves would be weak (like Peter) the teaching would be transmitted unscathed.

Jesus left His gifts of the seven sacraments whereby we can become holy. We would become children of God through Baptism. Our sins would be forgiven by the Sacrament of Penance and our souls nourished by the Eucharist. There would be high requirements expected of these Catholics and many would rebel and dissent from basics. Some would break off and create new forms of the ancient faith which would not be Catholicism but another form of Christianity. While thoughtful disagreement about policy was encouraged, rejection of revealed truth was not. Refusal of Christ's truth through His Holy Church, mainly the infrequent infallible teaching of the Pope, was considered heresy. To dismiss the Pope's teaching, even in an ordinary form, was considered theologically gauche. To split off from Christ's own Church was called schism.

One clear criterion to determine which group was heretical or schismatic or authentic was to search for the Bishop of Rome or the Pope. The old axiom was: *Ubi Petrus est, ibi ecclesia.* Where you find the Pope, you find the Church. God's will would be gleaned and taught from Sacred Scripture and the living tradition. And God's will is important for the serious Catholic. Our Catholic truth would be expressed through the teaching organ of the Church, the Magisterium, always under the protection of the Holy Spirit. Hence, serious positions of Christ's Church, even if not infallible, are to be taken seriously. A serious Catholic does not dismiss, out of hand, a strong if controversial global Catholic position on faith and morals but considers the position with respect and maturity before considering a legitimate disagreement. But the mature Catholic is exceedingly clear about the real Catholic Church. The marks are all there for those who can see. Pope Benedict XVI and his remark about studied ambiguity are of particular relevance here.

Meanwhile, we hear the chilling threats of dissidents telling us if we do not line up with their thought, millions will leave the Church abandoning her to become just another musty museum. How convenient to overlook the Lord's promise: "I am with you all days even unto the consummation of the world." And yet so intimidating! Fr. Ronald Knox, a brilliant English convert and son of the Archbishop of Canterbury, wrote, many years ago, of a future age when there would be a remnant of those Catholics who kept the faith and whose numbers greatly diminished in the face of outside pressures. They would keep the faith pure and untarnished to hand over to the Lord on His Second Coming. It is somewhat reflected in the Pope's vision of the creative minority whereby the Catholic stronghold (do we call it siege?) becomes highly unified and cohesive. Meanwhile, modern disagreements are not always respectful and issue-oriented but are often resulting in lamentable and vicious personal attacks on the messenger. This technique may have been borrowed from American dirty politics whereby one American attacks another, not on the issue, but on the person. Consult the Sen. Kennedy attack on the person of Sen. Santorum in the recent case of the ill woman in Florida.

To dismiss such latent apprehension might be naïve. In an interesting piece by Fr. Paul Mankowski, S.J. entitled, "Liberal Jesuits and the Late Pope," a point is made that there was widespread Wojtyla hatred in his Society (posted April 4, 2005, "No Sound Off"). He illustrates:

1. "I'd hear my Superiors pray that Wojtyla come to an early death…and go unrebuked in that jocular vein that signals sympathy."

2. Fr. Cyril Barrett, S.J. "[I]n a bellow that filled a London restaurant, 'The only thing wrong with that bloody Turk was that he couldn't shoot straight.'" (P. Mankowski assesses the remark: "Note that this is not the language of passionate disagreement, this is hatred, pure and simple.")

3. From a Jesuit academic: "The Society has not sold its soul to the restoration of John Paul II."

4. From a Jesuit Historian: "[H]e is not one of the worst popes: he's *the* worst. Don't misquote me."

The author claims that the reason for the hatred is no mystery. There is a pressure for doctrine to change. The venom of critics toward this charismatic Pope was the bitterest in the area where he differed least from his predecessors (and in which his successor will differ least from him) in repeating the truism that doctrine, being unchangeable, will not be changed. Mankowski suggests that these critics did the Pope an injustice in pretending that he is free to unpope himself by altering the deposit of Faith. Even the Protestant politician Newt Gingrich (now a Catholic convert) points out that the Pope being the Vicar of Christ can do nothing but speak the truth. He has no choice.

The dreams of the progressivists were frankly infantile. They were and are stunned that JPII didn't make their dreams come true. One thing we do know. What they clamor for is not the Catholic Church. They seek some kind of make-believe Church of their own making without which they will continue to seethe, no matter who is the Pope. Someone jested on a recent TV talk show that disaffected Catholics might join some other Church more to their liking where there are plenty of empty pews.

A similar kind of venom was spewed at Cardinal O'Connor when he was Archbishop of New York because he steadfastly taught official Catholic doctrine. This was unacceptable to many and hence he was caricatured and insulted regularly by those who wanted him to change Church teaching. The plan is to destroy the messenger if he will not change his message to suit the desires of the attacker.

In my own website, I often articulate what my Church teaches to the chagrin and fury of some of my readers. A recent e-mail to me read thusly: "Thank god [note the lower case] you are close to death [a reference to my eight-four years]. You are a superstitious Fascist. You write lies about a natural thing like homosexuality. Your Church is likewise dying. Ha ha!"

Another reader characterized me as a "mean spirited old man" after I had been interviewed in MSNBC by Ron Reagan Jr. and Monica Crowley in which I stated the simple and loving rationale of the Church towards the same-sex attraction tendency. I am an old bat and dinosaur but I have never been categorized as mean spirited by those who know me. But I plead for adult dialogue on the issue not on my character or on the character of Pope John Paul II or Cardinal O'Connor or anyone who sincerely tries to implement the Catholic teaching.

If one wishes for the real Catholic Church to stand up amid all the pretenders, one must look at the teachings and presence and traditions and indeed the theology and Scripture which Rome represents. But look and study the role of the Bishop of Rome, the Pope. Finally, if bias, prejudice and personal desires blind a person who seeks real fulfillment, it is

God's grace that helps one see the truth of Catholicism. A short cut to it: Seek the help of Mary, the Mother of the Lord, the patroness of Catholicism and ideal of women. She has helped many to inner peace and ultimate salvation.

What Do These Famous People Have in Common? The Search for the Single Human Common Denominator

What do the famous people, listed below, have in common? Apart from the demographic and empirical fact of belonging to the human race, they differ significantly in race, creed, culture, financial status, educational levels, nationality, age, talents, interests, hobbies, couture and cuisine styles, and myriad other variables. Is there anything one might find common to all these people? Perhaps it is a Rorschach test. Like looking at cloud formations and seeing what one wants to see. Or is it *quidquid percipitur, percipitur secundum modum percipientis.* Roughly translated, this means we see things through our own personal filters and so interpret them as reality. Let us look at this list and see what variable we find as a common denominator.

The List

Mother Teresa of Calcutta. Malcolm Muggeridge of the London Times and British Spy. Jackie Gleason, actor, humorist and philosopher. William F. Buckley, journalist and super conservative. Hugh Carey, Governor of New York State.

Governor John Volpe of Massachusetts. Governor Richard Hughes of New Jersey. Governor Malcolm Wilson of New York State. Al Capp, creator of Lil' Abner. Four-star General Alfred Gunther, prime military strategist of WWII and bridge expert.

Jim Farley, maker of American Presidents. Tommy Loughran, world's light heavyweight boxing champion. Anne Fremantle, English writer and spiritual leader. Robert

Rambusch, world class church architect. Cyril Ritchard, star of motion pictures, stage and television. Florence Henderson, Hollywood and television luminary. Miles Ambrose, New York Harbor Commissioner.

Bella Dodd, former Communist organizer. Archbishop Jakavos, Primate of Orthodox Catholics of North America. Rabbi Marc Tannenbaum, voice of Jewish thought in America. Elie Wiesel, Jewish writer and Holocaust survivor. George Sokolsky, Jewish journalist. Gene Ward, sportswriter. Bill Considine, sportswriter.

Harry Goz, as Tevyev in *Fiddler on the Roof.* Johnny Desmond, Broadway musical comedy star. David Susskind, television entrepreneur. David Merrick, Broadway producer. Frank Blair, NBC-TV commentator. Henry Cabot Lodge, diplomat and politician from Beverly, Mass. Thomas Melady, Ambassador to Burundi-Rwanda, and Uganda. Eamon Kennedy, Irish representative to the UN. Milton Monez, Portuguese representative to the UN. Mario Amadeus, Ambassador from Argentina to the UN. Dr. Alice Jourdain, Belgian philosopher and university professor. Dr. Detreich Von Hildebrand, German philosopher with international fame.

Norman Mailer, Pulitzer Prize winner and liberal philosopher. Ed McMahon of the *Tonight Show* and "heeeeere's Johnny." Mel Allen, the voice of the Yankees. Jeanne Dixon, famed psychic. Roy Wilkins, National Director of the NAACP. Dr. Ken Clark, famed psychologist who did early studies on psyches of black children and early race integrationist. Bricktop, grande dame of Rome's night life. Dizzy Gillispie, classic jazz trumpeter. Bayard Rustin, black leader in '60s and art collector.

All these and multitudes of others were interviewed on WNBC-TV by a balding, Jewish-Irish American priest, ME! During my television years at NBC, 30 Rockefeller Plaza, New

York City, from 1958 to 1973, I interviewed psychiatrists, psychologists, sociologists, and paleontologists from the University of Pennsylvania, political scientists from Johns Hopkins University, surgeons, educators, politicians, housewives, actors, diplomats and ordinary folk from the street.

Hence, commonality number one! They all, besides sharing basic human nature, experienced a television interview with an outright believer in God. And a further second variable found (through skillful questioning) was that all of them were seeking a stable and permanent meaning in their own lives. Even the very sophisticated and apparently totally self-sufficient showed glimmers of yearning. Sometimes, this quality was glossed over with hip talk and slight cynicism. But it was there if one had ears to hear. One hears the relevance of God.

A person of Faith simply nods in agreement and repeats the age-old wisdom of the great psychologist of Hippo, St. Augustine, who summed it all up thusly:

"Thou hast made us for thy self o God and our hearts are restless until they rest in Thee!"

The Wall of Separation: The Myth and Hoax

Many times, my religious views and those of countless others have been severely criticized for violating the sacred cow of the wall of separation between the state and religion. The putdowns we receive are usually delivered with the solemn tone and somber mien of the schoolmaster admonishing the rebellious student. This is the end of the matter: no further discussion; no adult dialogue. When I in my innocence would ask, where is such a separation described in the American jurisprudence, my betters, with a pained smile, will lecture me about the Constitution, the Bill of Rights, the Declaration of Independence, Justice Hugo Black, gobbledy-gook legalese and pure hokum.

Meanwhile, Justice Rehnquist, a reasonably well schooled constitutional law scholar, writes:

"There is simply no historical foundation for the proposition that the Framers intended to build the 'wall of separation' that was constitutionalized in Everson…. The 'wall of separation' between church and state is a metaphor based on bad history, a metaphor which has proved useless as a guide to judging. It should be frankly and explicitly abandoned."[4]

If this is so, how does one explain the widespread belief in this existent wall? Who advocates it? Where does it come from? Marc Levin, one of the more preeminent of contemporary constitutional lawyers, believes that the myth has been based on a misreading of a short courtesy note written by Thomas Jefferson to the Danbury Baptist Association in 1803. This note was written fourteen years after the Amendment was passed by Congress. It has been noted that he was not an ideal source of contemporary history relative to the meaning of the religion clauses of the First Amendment. He was not even in the United States when the Bill of Rights was passed by Congress. He was living in France. Yet, the critics still rely on Jefferson's words to justify their opposition to almost any government intersection with religion.

In a sense, the king has no clothes on. The freedom of exercise (of religion) clause clearly states that the government is prohibited from interfering with the people's free exercise of their own religion. It also prohibits the establishment of a national church having in mind the Church of England whereby a formal union of political and ecclesiastical authority was put in the hands of the state. There was no prohibition against religion but against a federal or national church. It is laughable when secular spokesmen quote Jefferson and Madison, the two most secular in outlook, to bolster current hostility to religion. Historically, the widespread belief, at that time, was that faith was a necessary predicate to liberty. We recall that it was Jefferson who wrote in the Declaration of Independence that all human beings have rights endowed, not by governments or monarchs, but by their Creator.

He also wrote, "...and can the liberties of a nation be thought secure when we have removed their only firm basis, a conviction in the minds of the people that these liberties are the gift of God?" And his colleague Madison, whose viewpoint is sometimes quoted as justification for separation, wrote that, "belief in God is essential to the moral order of the world." What does it take to enlighten our modern American that opposition to an established church is not opposition to religion in general. How did this truism become so lost to the today's secular minds? Madison further interpreted free exercise to mean no privileges and no penalties.[5] Interestingly, the very day after the First Amendment was proposed, the President was asked by Congressmen to issue a Thanksgiving to Almighty God for the blessings He had poured down upon them.[6]

What happened? How did viewpoints change so radically? How can one explain the contradiction between the history of the Republic with its clear intent and the modern near hostility to religion? The first 150 years of our history had multiple instances in which government monies were spent on sectarian religious causes. Note the considerable money spent on the Kaskasia Indians each year to support their Roman Catholic priests until 1897. However, in 1947, in the famous *Everson v. Board of Education* case, Justice Hugo Black started the separation question rolling. He wrote: "No tax in any amount, large or small, can be levied to support any religious activities or institutions, whatever they are called, or whatever form they may adopt to teach or practice religion." He continued, "The First Amendment has erected a wall between church and state. That wall must be kept high and impregnable. We could not approve the slightest breach."[7]

Marc Levin thinks that the Everson case is an inherently flawed opinion. He points out that the absolutist position leads to absurd outcomes and quotes Bruce Fein (once deputy attorney general of the United States) to make the point. "Black seemed to sense the absurdity of his categorical prohibition, which would have required public ambulances to deny service to a cleric who suffered heart attack while preaching from the pulpit. Accordingly, he immediately retreated from his unbending stance but without saying so."[8]

Justice Rehnquist describes the intellectual mess of separation thusly:

In the thirty-eight years since *Everson* our establishment clause cases have been neither principled nor unified. Our recent opinions, many of them hopelessly divided pluralities, have with embarrassing candor conceded that the "wall of separation" is merely a "blurred, indistinct, and variable barrier," which is "not wholly accurate" and can only be "dimly perceived."

What has apparently happened according to Judge Robert Bork and others is that the Court has intervened not on constitutional grounds but because it wishes to dictate policy. Even some members of Congress wrongly think of judges as policy makers.

It has been suggested that Black may have had more sinister reasons for his strange position. He was an ex-KKK member in the 1920s, a time when the Klan was fiercely anti-Catholic. Hugo Black junior and senior had negative feelings about the Catholic Church which they both suspected in the manner of Paul Blanshard whom they avidly read. The possibility of absurd conclusions (from the Black position) has surfaced many times. Note the 2000 Supreme Court decision on the prohibition of prayer before a football game based on "the right not to feel uncomfortable." Such nonsense now trumps the First Amendment's guarantee of the free exercise of one's religious feelings. Let us ask why so many Americans are displeased with *Roe v. Wade* after thirty years? One obvious reason is the dishonoring of the democratic choices of the people and the dishonoring of our basic religious rights. In the light of our democratic history and the clear will of the largely religious American populace, the contemporary meaning of this wall is absurd.

When human beings become driven by the absurd, they can contradict human nature itself. One might recall the tragic opinion of Roger Taney in *Dred Scott v. Sanford* in 1856. The humanity of slaves was denied in complete disregard of the more encompassing language of the Declaration of Independence which stated that "all men are created equal."

Such a conclusion derives from ignoring the very Natural Law of God Himself so enshrined in the Declaration. No one, in or out of office, can set himself above the divine law. Incidentally, neither John Kerry nor Ted Kennedy should feign surprise when they are called upon by the Church to use their persuasive gifts, for example, to reduce the incidence of abortion (a violation of both divine and natural laws), and certainly not to be its propagandists.

Douglas Kmiec, Professor of Constitutional Law at Pepperdine University, points out that the tools of interpretation are certainly the Constitution, text, history and structure. But one must remember, with Lincoln's insightful reflection, that the Constitution was framed for the philosophy of the of the Declaration, not the other way around. Government is instituted to ensure our unalienable rights which self-evidently come from God. Kmiec believes as a matter of original understanding that there is nothing in the Constitution to discourage religious people from urging government to agree with their public policy agenda. Stephen Carter, the noted Professor of Law at Yale makes the same point in his powerful book, *The Culture of Disbelief* (Basic Books, 1993).

On the other hand, did anyone censure a New York Senator when he, in effect, told an Alabama nominee to the Court of Appeals, that he could not be eligible for the judgeship since he was a believing Catholic? Does Article VI of the Constitution mean anything when it says: "No religious test shall ever be required as a Qualification to any Office or public Trust under the United States"? Dr. Charles Krauthammer, a noted physician and columnist, concluded that after the insulting appraisal by the Senator, henceforth no serious Catholic should ever be considered for a judgeship.

Whence the changes in religious freedom? We are told by fiery leftists that the Constitution is a living document which should be altered based on the preferences of individual judges in the light of new circumstances, like electronic wiretaps and the internet. But, Judge Stephen Markman, of the Michigan Supreme Court, tells us that our Constitution would be an historical artifact—a genuinely dead letter—if its original sense became irrelevant, to be replaced by the views of successive waves of judges and justices, who are intent on updating it with contemporary moral theory. Would such flexibility, deconstructionism and moral relativism feed even more into the obvious moral decay of our beautiful country? Is there any correlation between characterological breakdown and the contemporary perception of the wall of separation? There are many concerned American thinkers who believe this to be true.

There is something perennial about truth and goodness and God. Secularist groups legitimately have their own agenda but the original American political theory enshrines permanent religious values in its own meaning. Startling evidence of this is the Washington Monument, which was topped in 1888 by an aluminum cap with the words *Laus Deo* (praise be to God). On the 12th, 20th and 24th landings are biblical quotes and prayers carved into the stone. In 1848, a Bible was enclosed in the cornerstone, noting the moral direction and spiritual mood of America at that time. Even earlier, the Father of our country, George Washington, himself, with no apparent empathy with a wall of separation, prayed: "Almighty God, we make our earnest prayer that Thou will keep the United States in Thy Holy protection."

To paraphrase Cicero, even the stones shout out! It is obvious that the secular emperor has no clothes on! The wall is a myth and a hoax and, in the spirit of the late Justice Rehnquist, should be abandoned. Where is our modern Ronald Reagan who can eloquently shout: "Tear down that wall." Can we hear the words of the Lord Himself? "Unless the Lord builds the house, its builders labor in vain. Unless the Lord watches over the city, the watchman guards in vain." (Ps. 127).

I am old and tired but I love my country. I worry over it and pray for it. May the good God bless America and protect her from her own people!

The Difference Between Organized
Religion and Authentic Religion

The envelope addressed to me, marked personal and confidential, came from Vatican City with all kinds of official seals on it. With a bit of a cardiac tremor, I opened it and read the following opening line: "I am writing to you at the request of the Holy Father (Pope Paul VI)."

When the Pope was Cardinal Archbishop Montini of Milan, one of his dearest friends was an Italian Jewish intellectual named Max Ascoli. This intimate of the Pope emigrated to New York where he founded an influential and highly rated journal called *The Reporter*. In early 1964, Max Ascoli, the darling of the chic set, for some reason and unknown to *The New York Times*, decided to become a Catholic.

He wrote to His Holiness in Rome requesting help in this matter and by a series of strange convolutions, I, the half-Jew, the dirty neck from San Juan Hill in New York City, was selected for the challenging task of guiding this intellectual icon to the Baptismal font. With a faint and terrified heart, I recalled the story of G. K. Chesterton and his own road to Rome. The intellectual giant of English literature reportedly knocked on the door of the local Church to request instruction and reception into the Catholic Church. The local priest, simple and relatively unlettered, was likewise terrified at the request of the great GKC and stammeringly suggested to the caller that it might be more appropriate to contact the prestigious Jesuit House not far away. After all, they are the elite of the Church, the scholars and luminaries. G.K. asked the little cleric whether he believed the same doctrines which the Jesuits did. Upon a predictable positive reply from the country priest, G.K. said "I want you to instruct me." The rest is, as they say, history. God chooses the simple and the weak for His instruments, chosen not for their skills or charm but for His own great plan. I forthwith enthusiastically accepted Max Ascoli as my student.

He came twice a week for his lesson, arriving in a long, black chauffeur-driven limo. He was very tall, leaned unsteadily on a cane, and assessed me up and down with his one good eye in a kind of Long-John-Silver style. He sat opposite me in my little office and lectured me with a rich and deep grasp of Catholic history and theology. Throughout his superb presentations he inserted the phrase, "I love Chriiiiiiist," said with unmistakable sincerity through his heavy Italian accent. Recognizing that he knew more Catholic theology than I would ever know, I shortened his lessons and baptized him in the great church of St. Paul the Apostle in New York City.

Just after the ceremony, Max hugged me publicly in the Great Italian *abbraccio* and said for all to hear: "Father, you must excuse me. I am Italian. I am anti-clerical." His remark did not and does not upset me. I was, too, and am, on some levels, anti-clerical even though I am a cleric myself. This position is that of the Pope Benedict XVI variety who, as scholars are discovering, is in the Curia but not of the Curia. The distinction is significant. This Pope does not have the careerist logic which so many others cherish. Nor does he view life and the Church and religion primarily through the prism of curial politics or bureaucratic logic. Rather, he stands back and approaches life and problems objectively on the basis of genuine conversation with principles, not rigid preconceptions. This insight is taken from the recent book by John Allen Jr. called *The Rise of Benedict XVI* (Image, 2007).

And its application can be enormously important for a balanced Catholic spirituality. I remember my extreme irritation in the eternal city of Rome when a paunchy, sullen priest, in his food-stained soutane and his ridiculous round hat, elbowed me in a crowded bus. I was nauseated by this organized religion symbol. I am angered by the arrogant, white cuffed clerical personnel of the various bureaux (called dicasteries in the Vatican) who dispense permissions and favors as if they were the lords of some medieval fiefdoms. I am sickened by the ambitious cleric who longs to wear the purple or some mark of distinction to prance around sanctuaries like a strutting popinjay.

Of course, I know of the homosexual priest who has used his exalted status to prey sexually on teen aged boys and of underdeveloped priests who have exploited naïve women. I know of drunken priests and power-crazy priests and egotistical priests. I know lazy priests and ineffectual ones.[9] But I also know what Graham Greene describes in his classic book *The Power and the Glory*. The glory of Christ's priesthood is carried in weak vessels of clay; a priesthood which is powerful and beautiful and loving. Greene's priest is a drunk who fathers a child, who wrings pesos out of poor peasants but who can offer the Eucharistic sacrifice of the Mass, absolve the sinner, and teach people how to pray.

I knew a priest in the Balearics who was paid by the state. He was bored, lazy and empty and did the Mass mechanically because it was a job. He was despised by the local community which was largely uneducated and simple but hungering for a lively faith and not getting It. They had religion. He had organization. Anti-clerical? In this instance I certainly am. Yet, my religion teaches me that even he was a valid conduit of God's grace through the great sacramental system provided by the Catholic Church which I love and defend.

I know the Catholic Church has miscreants, both clerical and lay. But I know this Church is the one of the second chance, the Church of mercy and forgiveness. It has been said that the Catholic Church is not a museum of saints but a clinic for sinners. The Church is not self-absorbed, puffy, red-faced clerics with piggy eyes. Nor is it the superficial uninformed social Catholic who might go to Mass on Sunday for human reasons. Perhaps there are hypocrites who go to Sunday Mass to show off their couture or to exhibit how reverently they carry their Bibles like some lens-lice politicians. But without any rash judgment I know that there are scores of decent and honest Catholics who worship God and not organizations. Their reasons for attending Mass are honorable and adult.

I am aware of the we-are-the-Church attitude wherein every shade and level of Catholic wants a share of the control and policies of the Church. Clearly, on some level this is true. On another, it is not. The Church is the faith of history, articulated by the Pope, Christ's Vicar. It is the Sacraments, the vital prayer life, the rich Catholic tradition and the confident dependence on the Holy Spirit which has suffused and guided this Church for hundreds of years. This is authentic religion. It is about loving and obeying God. One honestly cannot blame religion if neurotics twist God's love into hatred. How often I have heard the superficial remark that religion causes wars and holocausts. 9/11 was not caused by religion but by sick minds which distort and pervert. Sick accretions and narcissistic trappings belong to the organization and not essentially to Christ's Church. During the painful scandal exposures of 2002, Fr. Benedict Groeschel CFR, a noted and valiant champion of Catholicism, said that he would never defend the over-bureaucratized offices of the Vatican but only Jesus. In effect, he distinguishes between the organized Church which can, at times, be corrupt and the authentic Church. One cannot in conscience defend the indefensible. Don't even try!

That some Archbishop in Ireland fathered a son and supported him for years with Church money or that some high-ranking Monsignor in New York will imprudently squire a married woman around to his fancy summer home or that some ambitious pastor will steal from parish finances for his membership fees in elegant clubs angers and saddens me. But how can it affect my faith? What have those things to do with my belief system? Apart from my emotional distress, these things of the organized Church have nothing to do with me. Those people have to answer to God for what they do. I have to answer for my own misdeeds, not theirs.

Of course, we are angered, enraged, and feel betrayed by the sinful behaviors of leaders we have trusted. Yet, it seems hypocritical of the non-churchgoers to gleefully point their fingers at human weakness as they, the accusers, now try to justify their own miscreant behavior which caused them to leave the Church in the first place. I don't think it is cynical to recall the brilliant insight of Sigmund Freud and his highlighting the alleged-motivation question. The human psyche will allege that the primary reason one acts as one does is a highly noble and rational one. For example, one might say: *I leave the Catholic Church because of all the hypocrites in it and all the stupidity and the insensitivity of its leaders. However, my real reason is that I am conflicted between the stringent requirements of the Church and my own desires for forbidden behaviors such as abortion or the homosexual lifestyle among others.* A nice convenient emotional juggling act! But as it is with phonies in the organized religion crowd so is it with the finger pointers. Hypocrisy and lying to oneself eventually come home to roost.

In the words of the old time talk show host, Jack Paar, "Let's be honest." The motivations for evil behavior are not religious but psychological. The beautiful motivations of authentic religion do not lead to wars and persecution. Distorted and underdeveloped psyches do. Don't preach to me about religious wars and the wild-eyed shouting of Salem witch-hunting ministers or clerics of the Inquisition or fiery incantations of imams. Let us use our intellects and make distinctions. Authentic religion—let us support and practice it. Let us name distortion for what it is.

As for Max Ascoli, when he, the anti-clerical, was dying, he sent for me that he might receive the Sacrament of Healing, then called Extreme Unction. He met his God as a truly religious man, fully believing in the fullness of revelation in Catholicism maintaining his autonomy as an educated, intelligent and adult man. Perhaps, the clue is that he was grown up and had no need to prolong adolescent rebellion. Max Ascoli, in the opinion of this Jewish, Irish, Catholic priest, is a credible model of imitation. I am delighted with the Catholic faith, and I do enjoy my freedom to be a rational anti-clerical.

The Goodness of Catholic Priests

Recently, forty-three good men, mostly Catholic priests and a few deacons, spent four days together in a seaside retreat house in New Jersey, seeking a deeper relationship with their God and searching for better ways to serve His people. There were grizzled, wrinkled, battered veterans among them (one with an oxygen tank to keep him alive and a few others on canes to relieve the crippling pain of arthritis). There were young, wide-eyed, bushy-tailed rookie priests and still others in between.

As a participant-observer, I saw in them a touching, simple, direct piety which I rarely see. I watched these forty-three good men, attentive and humble, as they listened to the presentations of a brother-priest, the retreat master. Uncritically, they gratefully drank in his words in their wish for an expansion and growth of their own priesthood. I watched them as they sat in the chapel during their free time. Their reverence and devotion to their Eucharistic Lord was patent. There was no doubt as to their belief in the Real Presence of Jesus before them. The silence in that chapel, while profound, was deafening with the vibrations of faith.

I saw one young priest kneeling before a huge outdoor crucifix, his eyes fixed on the image of Jesus, unembarrassed, utterly oblivious to his surroundings. The uncomplicated sincerity of this scene brought a gulp to my throat. I saw priests deep in contemplation, gazing out over the sea, with an invisible but plain sign saying "Don't enter. Talking with God." I saw others walking up and down the little boardwalk with their rosaries dangling from their hands, petitioning Mary, the Mother of Christ, the Blessed Virgin and mother of priests for honesty and authenticity in the priesthood.

I listened to a former and successful radio announcer describe the draw to priesthood away from the phoniness and glitz of modern media. I listened to a former professional baseball player (and now a pastor) speak concretely and directly how the Lord called him from the diamond to the sanctuary. I listened to raspy, untrained but loving voices as they sang praise to Christ in the concelebrated Masses. I heard a young priest pray aloud that we might know how much we help Him to carry His cross by bravely carrying our own and uniting our pain to His.

Is it the hand of God I felt when, immediately upon arrival, the mysterious brother-priest bond became so palpable? Did I not feel this in every mission and hamlet I visited in Africa with any priest I met? African, Irish, English, Dutch, German, American, Spanish, any priest? These men I had just met, fairly shrieked out a vibe that they knew that they were somehow special to God. Somehow, I sensed that this self-awareness could be shared in its fullness only with a brother priest.

There was, consequently, a refreshing absence of the New Age posturing of "we are all the same." Collaterally, there was a unique kind of joy which is unlikely in a more heterogonous society. This joy was pervasive and unlike other gatherings I have attended. We could all afford, in this climate, to openly assent to *Lumen Gentium* (no. 8) with the Church's distinction that Holy Orders confers a priesthood different from that of Baptism not only in degree but in kind. One could sense this self-awareness even if it was seldom articulated. These men knew that Holy Orders conferred on them alone a special dimension of Christ's own personal power. These priests were awed by what they are and humbly grateful for being chosen. In this pervasive climate there was no need for pretense or sex-sensitive diplomacy. There was no pressure to placate the shrill voices of special interest groups.

The message streaming from the physical setup and the roster of the participants was apparent: "We are men set apart." It is that very realization which clarifies the obligation to be holy and to be faithful and brave shepherds and leaders. The retreat climate, temporarily at least, freed these men of God from any fear of being called elitists because they know the truth, deep within themselves. Priests are different. During this retreat they were able not only to face the truth but to tell themselves that it is the truth of Christ which ultimately and alone saves anyone. These men were able to be truly honest with themselves this week and to admit their deep inner conviction about being a priest. They admit that it is not basically doing that matters. It is basically being that matters. There is a being about the priesthood which is uniquely special. It is even ontological.

This brave and honest point they saw and admitted. They are other Christs. And other Christs in a way only they possess. Let us be honest. Priests are broken, vulnerable vessels but they have a power no one else has. Does anyone dispute this claim? The more a priest knows who he really is and what he really is, the more priestly, under God, he becomes. Being aware of the spiritual mark, the character, the branding is more conducive to real priesthood than all the techniques and mechanisms drummed up by ecclesiastical public-relation shills. Facial tics and body language are important to assess but more profoundly, even more pragmatically, it is primary to know, "what happened to me when I was ordained."

This goodness sample of the forty-three might well be generally representative of the priesthood as a whole. The two to four percent of evil priests is saddening and serious but statistically minimal. I am tired of special interest lobbyists throwing in my face the infrequent example of the wayward bishop or the thieving monsignor or the predatory priest as if these were norms. Would that this frenetic critic had been at this retreat and had seen the true character of priests. Did he show the same zeal at the faults of Jewish and Protestant leaders? Or the abominable failures of teachers in the public schools? Why the gleeful rushing to publicize the occasional failure of Catholic clerics and not those of other groups? Is it because our failures are relatively rare? The Bishop of Bridgeport thought so, years ago, when the *Thorn Birds* made such a big splash. Bishop Curtis then noted: "It is sensational because it is so unusual. This does not apply to most priests." The forty-three say amen to that. Perhaps there is some subtle and hidden agenda for the media. Envy or bigotry and evil? Who knows?

However, the goodness which the forty-three signify is the true norm of Catholic priests. By its own weight and power, this very goodness will defuse any attempt to defame Christ's own priesthood. The streetwise Catholic knows this through the *sensus fidelium* (the instinct of the faithful). Despite the turbulence of public scandal, the Catholic Church will more than survive. For those who might unnecessarily worry, a little peek into a priests' retreat (anywhere) will more than dissipate the negatives about our Priests. Goodness is from God, and goodness is overflowing in the Catholic Priesthood. You can bet on it.

Is Morality Generational or Innate?

The twenty-two-year-old was wholesome looking and a recent Catholic college graduate. He spoke with total confidence and knowledge about this mystery called life. He was fully aware, he said, of the difficulties that others may have had but he felt in complete control. He had his life all planned out, disregarding the loving advice and concern of his parents and somewhat old-fashioned friends. He sat in my office and with unshakeable élan described the blueprint of his life. He had a lover to whom he was committing himself for life. He just knew that this was it. This was real. This was obviously forever. As he spoke with typical inexperienced certitude, there was something troublingly bland about him with even a slight hint of trance

They met three months prior and were so comfortable with each other. It was all so different from his awkward and dishonest attempts at heterosexual liaisons. They would be so happy together, traveling, surf boarding and eating at fantastic restaurants. He felt sheer bliss. Idealistic love was available for him. Physical pleasures were only part of his soaring delight. Finally and at last, he was comfortable in a relationship, sharing a common love.

The devastation of his parents was insignificant to him. It was regrettable but a mere temporary unpleasantness which would eventually evaporate when they realized how happy he was and how correct his decision was. After all, if they really loved him, they would rejoice in his happiness. It would take a little time but with some patience on his part, they would come around to his view and accept his life partner. They would get over it. As would his siblings and their children. He was astonished that they thought there was something bad about "gay" living. But, again, after all, they were from another generation while his generation is more liberated and enlightened and which, of course, knows that homosexual love is basically the same as heterosexual love. Values and attitudes change, he said, and he was living in modern times. His parents and others simply would have to accept that fact. (Obviously, this unreal infatuation state of being is not limited to the homosexual world. It has been repeated endlessly and historically in the heterosexual world as well.)

His sole reason in meeting with me was to placate his parents who, broken hearted, hoped that I would be able to persuade him to delay his decision. To them living the homosexual life was unnatural, toxic and sinful. Their profound love for him was the very reason for their suffering; they saw him, their very flesh and blood, seriously considering a self-destructive life. For my part, I found a young man totally brainwashed. He would not even consider views different from his own. He was completely closed minded. He spoke only to those who held views like his. In his mind, there was no other option. No other way. Hard statistics on the failures of homosexual unions were brushed aside as irrelevant. Clinical experiences were discounted in the light of the decline in heterosexual marital stability. That he would be excluded from the Eucharist was passed over quickly and easily because his progressive-minded priest mentors had implied that God understands—and besides his love for his partner would compensate, should there be any ritual deprivation. The Church, he claimed was not with the times and one could confidently anticipate that future thinking would ultimately coincide with his own. Today's Catholics, if they are current, think for themselves and decide what is right and wrong. They are freed from the priest culture of previous times. So the thinking goes.

The basic point for him is that notions of right and wrong are generational. His own generation has different values and the older less enlightened one really has to come to terms with the modern realities. There is no such thing as eternal or perennial morality. Everything changes. Shades of Heraclitus and his everything-is-in-flux theory. Whatever happened to Parmenides and his theory of permanence? Where is the balance between permanence and change we so ardently desired? Some things never change. Some things do. And there is a gray moral area. Perhaps, it takes maturity and good sense to know the difference and nuance implied in the famous Serenity Prayer: "God, grant me the serenity to accept the things I cannot change, courage to change the things I can, and wisdom to know the difference." The sportswriter, Ray Kerrison, once wrote semi-jocosely that when God gave the Ten Commandments to Moses, He reminded His man on earth that these laws were forever and would not expire in 2005. Some things never change even though adaptation and progress often occur.

Alleged motivations are commonplace with human beings. There is more here than the eye can see. This is not merely intellectual confusion. This is a huge emotional problem which is not solvable by logic or facts. Nor is it easy to face. This young man hungers for something he believes is unavailable to him but which he illusions can be gained by perversion. He must rationalize in order to go ahead with his tragic plan.

However, the superficial and sad approach to life described above is not limited to naïve and inexperienced young people. I have a priest client from somewhere who is sixty-six-years-old, is deeply loved by his people and who is profoundly addicted to male porno on his computer. His addiction is progressive which factor contributes to the noticeable decline in the spiritual life of his parish. A parish employee who discovered the secret by accident, properly and lovingly confronted the priest who instantly denied any knowledge of the origin of these data, claiming that someone else must have done it. It was the old Genesis game of passing the buck. Someone else is to blame. I am innocent. Meanwhile, the priest is doctrinally orthodox and is the chaplain for the regional Courage apostolate, a national movement to help homosexual Catholics strive for the mandated virtue of Chastity. He seemed to have two faces, one for the parish and one for his secret vice.

Further information and data, however, revealed his deep enmeshment in this sick and perverted behavior. He would spend up to five hours engrossed with the enchantment even seeking online membership in an organization giving him access to young males.

In a discussion with his employee, he insisted that there are far more serious affronts to God's will than mere sexual lapses. It was the tired centuries old game of rationalization. He listed the usual litany of intolerance, racism, social injustice, sexism and homophobia. I have heard so many patients argue that this sexual behavior is necessary to relieve sexual tension. It is not hurting anyone. (Shades of John Donne and his, "No man is an island") It relieves loneliness. It compensates for not having a wife. Everyone is doing it. We are more adult these days and have dropped the old-time rigidity. We have new values and deeper understanding of human nature. And endless variations on the theme. The old attempt to ennoble the ignoble by justifying one evil by another.

Yet, way down deep in his soul, he knows that his behavior is evil, that he pollutes his priesthood, and that he betrays his people. He knows he distances himself from his God. Yet, he digs himself deeper and deeper into a vortex of misery. How did this ever happen?

In the beginning, intellectual seduction. The smart ones talk of deconstructionism, that there are no essences, that nothing really is absolute, that everything is relative and so on and so on. Someone holds that it is all right to so behave because, well, just pick any reason. Anything will do. Little step by little step until, with repeated microbehaviors, one is hooked. It is now necessary to construct a mental mechanism to justify what one really knows to be destructive.

The young twenty-two-year-old and the sixty-six-year-old are doing the same thing. They have been seduced by the demonic idea that morals change with the times. It is no longer necessary to struggle with inner conflict which no one finds desirable. We note that this is substantially different from mores. In effect, the Holy Father, Pope Benedict XVI, sees this point with great clarity: i.e., the burning issue of the times is the battle for objective truth. He knows well, as do those of us of the Greatest Generation, that relativism leads to Dachau.

The young man and the priest are terribly important in their own right but an even wider question arises. The survival of civilized living. Only a form of Christianity clear in its own beliefs and its system of authority will have the inner strength to stand up against such alien forces which are attempting to hijack or seduce the world. The two sad illustrations noted above are symptoms of what is brewing. Is it any wonder that observant ones are concerned? May St. Michael, the enemy of Lucifer, protect us!

A Jewish Agnostic's Discovery of Her God

She was an incredibly bright young copy writer for a leading ad agency with responsibility for the Ford account but writhing under an agony of spiritual emptiness. Though Jewish by ethnicity, she was totally lacking any kind of religious anchor. Written over forty years ago, her self-report, which follows, illustrates a fascinating journey from the darkness of not knowing to the joy of arriving.

Notes—Mid-Journey

I began this journey unprepared. I had no chance to consider, let alone inquire, what the standard things to take along might be. It is probably just as well, because they're not the sort of thing you can readily lay your hands on. And although I have not reached my destination yet—or know for certain that I shall get there—I wouldn't have missed this trip for the world. Besides, truly experienced travelers may be right when they say that all you really need to take along is the right spirit, particularly when it's an unplanned trip. When I set out, that November Tuesday not three months ago, I had no idea I was going anywhere.

Indeed, I was well on my way before I realized just where I might be headed. So far as I knew, the only place I was going that first evening was to sit in on a class in Catholic instruction.

I never would have gone alone. A friend of mine was taking the course as a refresher before being baptized into the Church she had accepted four years earlier. Since she had every intention of going alone, this doesn't say anything about why I went. Except that if she had not, I would not have. But she also went to California last year, and it never occurred to me to tag along. Chalk it up, if you like, to a mind uncomfortably atrophied from disuse, or to idle curiosity, or to the finger of grace delivering an almost imperceptible nudge to an unsuspecting shoulder. Does it matter much now how I came to that first night? I do know I meant to go only that once, or perhaps twice. I certainly didn't mean to register for the course. But the woman behind the reception desk assumed—with ample justification, to be sure—that anyone who was there was there for precisely that purpose. So I filled out the card she handed me, feeling the same dull edge of guilt one feels when one accepts an indefinite invitation to visit someone one has no intention of seeing again. I knew I felt uncomfortable; I had no idea how uncomfortable until my sub-conscious acted up and I couldn't remember my telephone number, which was one of the harmless-seeming bits of information the card called for. I had to ask my friend, adding with a laugh of sorts, "Don't call us, we'll call you."

The class was quite large; there were twenty-five, perhaps thirty people there. Bent upon doing the greatest good for the greatest number, I expect, the priest translated Catholicism into everyday terms for us. In this way, the miracles became God's *Good Housekeeping* seal of approval of Christ. Similarly, rejecting the validity of the Church's authority and teachings because individual clerics happened to be notably fallible amounted to throwing out the baby with the bath water. My knowledge of theology was pathetically meager; yet I sensed that Catholicism was losing something in the translation. At times, I felt that what we were getting was not only freely translated, but also was an incomplete and perhaps even expurgated version of the story. We were told a good many facts about the Church, but the priest, I became increasingly convinced, was not about to go into its essence; he was, I felt, beating about the burning bush, so to speak.

This life-size church could not be the giant that had captured the allegiance of John Henry Newman? Would Gerard Manley Hopkins have subjugated his rare gift to so down-to-earth a Church? Would its resurgence through the Oxford Movement have terrified Anthony Froude? Would, indeed, so matter of fact a faith arouse the intellectuals of that generation—and others, including her own—to such fierce partisanship. There had to be more to Catholicism than this! We were, I felt, circling the core. Its essence was not being communicated to us. Any more than not seeing communicates the essence of blindness. You don't have to be blind to see that. Nor did I have to have the Catholic faith to know that its essence transcended literal definition. Surely, I felt—as must the youngster who, having often heard it said that *Moby Dick* is the great American novel, finds himself with the classic comics version—surely, this isn't the real thing, surely there must be another version.

During the third week of the course, we heard about another version. A friend of Janet knew of another course in Instruction, about which she had heard good things. It was given by the Paulist Fathers. Feeling we had little to lose, we changed courses at that point along the road.

Even before we turned up for the first lecture there, I found out one thing about the Paulist priest with whom we were to study that put me on my guard. This father was like a bold-face sign in a language you can't read, but which you have a vague feeling says stop! His name was Father James B. Lloyd. Which doesn't hint at what he told Janet when she called to arrange our transfer into his class. Janet told him that she would be coming with a Jewish friend who was interested—but not in converting. That, Father Lloyd replied, was fine. Incidentally, he asked Janet, did she know that he was Jewish?

We had both known only that I was Jewish; and only I had known how Jewish. Not that my family were religious Jews. They never took me to a synagogue. But I was at home with Jewishness as my parents knew it and instilled it in me. In accordance with their view, they taught me Yiddish and Jewish history and introduced me to Yiddish literature. Cultural identification—propagation of their culture—was their way of expressing their conviction that, in a world where Jews, even the most assimilated who conscientiously wanted no part of their Jewish heritage, might die because in the eyes of Gentiles they remained, then and forever, Jews. In such a world, my parents felt, one must live as a Jew. Then, if one were to die at Gentile hands, it would be because one had more of Jewishness than Jewish blood.

My father died when I was nine; my mother when I was eighteen. After her death, I sought a new center. Because I no longer had someone to belong it, I sought something. And I sought it first in the observance of Judaism. But I was only made to feel my aloneness more severely; perhaps because there is so much of Jewish ritual a woman cannot perform. I did not find the sense of community, the comfort, or the direction that I was looking for. My sense of cultural identification did not increase; neither did it lessen. It seemed unrelated to the religious observance that I continued to walk through.

Thus, I came to the first class with the priest who said he was Jewish. This man in the clerical collar was not devoted to the popularization of his Faith. He was, in his mid-thirties, and often looked younger for enthusiasm. This enthusiasm he offered without modification, but one sensed (also without working at it) to his class. He offered them, as well, precision, succinctness, directness. He laughed easily. He often gestured broadly, not always consciously one felt, to indicate the enormousness of the universal Church—flashing rather extravagant cufflinks in the process. He conveyed a distinct sense of strength, reinforced but not based upon his physical bearing. Above all, although not oppressively apparent, was his contentedness. And, of course, there was the Jewishness. This last poked at the forefront of my mind again and again. I had for many years been self-conscious about my being Jewish; now I began to be self-conscious about his being Jewish.

I found myself making asides to Janet. When Father Lloyd made a particularly erudite point, I remarked that it was his Jewish half speaking. We speculated on his name. It was so blatantly not a Jewish name. Might the middle initial "B" stand for Bernie? My somewhat tasteless comments paled but persisted before my increasing suspicion that this man might be a threat to my position in that class—to my observer status. Surely one of the major obstacles to a Jew's conversion to Catholicism is a fear of cultural betrayal—of forsaking his people, of negating their ofttimes bare survival. This fear did not up and leave me; but it was quelled by the very fact of this man's vocation. That he was a Jewish priest did not refute the notion of betrayal, but it did refute its inevitability. I was not on the verge of an instant conversion; I was a million light years or so away. But I knew then that if anyone could bring about my conversion this priest was that man. I was dismayed but not enough to turn back lest I be confronted with the rightness of his faith.

Amid this turmoil, a thousand questions unanswered, a hundred new doubts and self-doubts vying for my attention and his help, Christmas came. We had come into Father Lloyd's class toward the end of a course, I knew, and the fact that it didn't coincide with the other course we had begun presented no great difficulty to my mind. But the fact that the course was now over did. A new course wouldn't begin until mid-January. I wondered whether I'd come back then. But what I really wondered about was that they didn't see how foolhardy it was to give me this month in which to reconsider the wisdom of prolonging this journey into unknown country. I had not counted on midnight Mass. My going there was not, of itself, unusual. I had been going to midnight service for more than ten years. And I had almost always chosen a Catholic Church to go to on Christmas Eve, because of the music, because of the pomp, because the worshippers seemed so much more, well, involved than in a Protestant Church.

I had, I recalled, envied them their involvement. But I had not begrudged it. Any more than I begrudge their voices to the children in grade school who could sing, who didn't have to be a listener like me. It didn't lessen the attraction music had for me. But it did make me feel an outsider, it did make me feel inadequate. It did make me feel keenly that I was ungifted. At Mass, too, I had always felt ungifted; as if God's gift of faith were, like singing, a talent I didn't have.

From the beginning this midnight Mass was special. I had heard the Paulist Choir before; but never had their song seemed to transcend the star-embellished roof of the Church and reach for the real stars beyond. We had excellent seats. Before, I had always kept to the side and toward the back, reluctant to displace those who really belonged. I felt no such reservations this night and used my vantage point wholeheartedly. I took in everything, the festive altar, the flock of nuns, the priests of the order who, not participating in the Mass, came in singing and in pairs and took seats in the front pews. It was some time before I began to get jittery. Father Lloyd was not among the non-participating priests. Nor did he appear in front of the altar with the priests who were about to begin Mass. I felt loss grip me: my precarious tie with this place was fast slipping apart. Mass began. I tried to concentrate, in vain. It was full fifteen minutes after Mass began that Father Lloyd slipped down a side aisle and back toward the sacristy. When he emerged, it was to pass in front of the altar, genuflect, then continue past the front of the Church and up the other side aisle. Only then did it dawn on me: he was to give the talk!

It was a sober talk, long for a midnight Mass sermon. It was also cautionary. Father Lloyd talked about the tangents on which we stray from the central theme of Christmas—from its only real point. Then he extended his arm and wrist and hand and forefinger toward the crèche at the front of the church, until he seemed to touch the infant in the cradle, and he said: "That baby is God." He had said it slowly. And then he said it once more. "That baby is God." And then there He was. For a second I would have sworn He was there.

The moment of recognition was fleeting. But I knew I had felt it. The way you know you have felt pain, even after it has gone and you cannot recapture its intensity: A shadow of its quality remains. Outside the Church, Mass over, I teased my friends. Did they know that it was my beginner's luck that accounted for the fact that Father Lloyd, out of some forty priests in that home base of the Paulists, had been chosen to give the talk? I did not mention my moment of recognition to them. What could I have charged that up to? And the other things. Little things. Like the time Father Lloyd said, "Do you know what we would say today if someone made the claims Christ did? We'd say: 'Who does He think He is, Almighty God?'"

I thought it was a genuinely witty point and repeated it around. In a day or two I noticed that people's laughter was great in proportion to their devoutness. My avowed atheist and agnostic friends laughed little more than politely. Then I realized: it was really an inside joke. And since when was I inside enough to get Father Lloyd's joke? A little thing, to be sure, but then how does one size up a growing comfort in Church? Does one credit the quiet in an empty church with my sense of peace there? With my inclination to pause for breath there? I live alone; my apartment is as quiet as I like, and I generally keep either the phonograph or radio on when I am not watching TV. A little thing? Not in my eyes. Not now. And especially not during those weeks between classes when the peace was bright shining new and sustained me.

For the first time, I could glimpse faith, even though it wasn't right in front of my eyes. For the first time, I felt, rather than knew, what these two lines by George Herbert are all about: "Methought I heard One calling, Childe;/And I reply'd, My Lord."

No, Faith had not burst forth full blown within me. But I felt the stirrings, like a half-grown fetus in the womb makes itself felt, declares its intention to be born—and to live.

My disinterest had vanished. My interest had not only grown, but it had also altered. I knew now that I had a real stake in the classes. Not quite like Saint Joan's, I joshed myself, but of half the same shape. Without being able to pin down a moment in time, I had become committed. Not to the Church. But to the course of instruction, to following the road upon which I was still and repeatedly surprised to find myself, until the end. To see what might be there for me. When classes began again, I went with more enthusiasm than equilibrium. My faith was shakier than a newborn colt: it clearly could not stand on its own two feet. It wavered; it collapsed. But my faith in my self-sufficiency, in my ability to go on without faith, was shakier still.

That first class was the hardest. It still is. The lecture was about the existence of God. I was not about to deny God's existence at this juncture. But I wasn't interested in not denying Him; I wanted to affirm him. And it was a strange God whom Father Lloyd confronted us with. A God of Justice. A God of Justice *cum* mercy even that I could comprehend. But a loving God. Or, to pin down the problem precisely, a God who loved me. If this were the God of Abraham—let alone the God of Job—He must have undergone a successful analysis, to have become so much less exacting, so much more giving. What Father Lloyd and what the Church faced me with was a God who seemed too good to be true.

That week I went out and bought a medal of St. Jude. Which seems to me to say more about possibility than impossibility.

I had been going to Mass, but not regularly. The only thing I had been doing consistently—religiously, so to speak—were attending class and listening to the Sunday morning interview broadcasts Father Lloyd mediated. And then, the last Sunday of the current series, I found myself with a choice to make. There was a special Mass that morning, in celebration of the conversion of St. Paul. In order to attend, I would have to miss half the broadcast, half the last broadcast for months.

I went to the Mass. It was a Pontifical Mass and quite exciting to see. But I think I was excited as much by my decision as by the ceremony. I had to recognize the milestone. The Mass meant more to me than the program. And I could see beyond; I was not, irrevocably bound to celebration about Catholicism; Father Lloyd was no longer my sole tie with St. Paul's.

That evening I was at the movies. During the second feature I became restless. I wanted to be off; I wanted to be in church. I left the movie theatre and hurried to Blessed Sacrament, our parish church. That evening, for the first time, I touched my right knee to the floor.

That was a week ago, I go nearly every day to church now. But, how often I go to church is less relevant, it seems to me, than how far I must yet go—to the Church. Damascus is still beyond my horizon. When I go to bed, the agnostic's prayer is still the one I say. When I kneel then, it is to tell God that, I cannot yet imagine His loving me, I am willing to try. And I am more than willing to know and love Him. God willing.

Fr. Lloyd's Epilogue

Ultimately, she was baptized into the Catholic faith and became the prototype of the ideal lay Catholic. She was a daily communicant, deep into parish activities and generally the kind of Catholic that the Church hopes to see in this world. However, she met a famous theologian from a prestigious religious order and fell deeply in love with him. They married with the intent to show, by leadership and example, what the ideal Catholic couple should be. In time, the gloss dissipated and their marriage broke up. Her interest in and quest for the spiritual life continued, however, and she found ethnic and spiritual rest in Judaism. She sees her quest as going from agnosticism to Catholicism which helped her to find God and finally to Judaism. Her affection and respect for Catholicism continues even to this day. I, as her instructor who baptized her a Christian, can understand her journey. Being half Jewish I know the great pull to the people we call Jews, God's chosen ones. She even now believes in transubstantiation as an insight to the Holy Eucharist but feels truly at home at last. Is there any other response than wishing her God's blessing and peace now that she is seventy years old?

Is There Really Such a Thing as Happiness?

During the crushing times of the Great Depression, my financially restricted family patronized a local grocery store run by a man we respectfully called Mr. Thompson. He was a very important person in our neighborhood because he supplied us with the needed cold cuts, veggies, milk and butter. As it often happens in times of social stress, we had great community solidarity. Everyone was poor—or so we thought. Everyone was struggling just to survive. And we were impressed with Mr. Thompson's formidable skills in running his food emporium. And, further, we, with our rough New Yawkese, were awed at his fancy New Hampshire accent whenever, with his loose-fitting dentures, he discussed Shakespeare and classical literature. Although he wore a battered old gray fedora all year, a long dirty apron (like the waiters in the paintings of Lautrec) and glasses that kept slipping down his nose, we thought he was very cultured.

He had come to New York seeking his fortune and wound up running a tiny food supply store and living in a walk up, third floor, cold water flat. He worked six days a week and saved Sundays for his passion and enjoyment—reading. I recall when I was a high school sophomore just beginning to marvel at the joy of books, he mesmerized me with a recap of Goldsmith's "Deserted Village" which he had read the day before. His eyes sparkled and his voice vibrated with palpable joy as he shared this classic with a dirty-necked kid from the streets. He had had a happy Sunday. I was struck by this. An old man with very little of this world's goods can sit huddled by a primitive stove in a near slum and experience something of what every single human being wants—happiness. How can this be?

I had been raised in the world of the pragmatic. Get a good job, preferably a city job. Move out of this seedy neighborhood. Study only that which will help you get more money. Don't study useless stuff like poetry or philosophy. Material security is what really matters. Save for your old age. Watch out for your pennies and the dollars will watch out for you.

Endless were those admonitions. And it made great sense in the terrible world of the early 20th century where hunger and street evictions were commonplace. But even in the world of the 21st century where opulence abounds and potbellied stoves are a quaint reminder of an earlier and more restricted era, we see such throwback examples as the Citibank highway signs: "Money can't buy you happiness but it can buy marshmallows which is kinda' the same thing." Energy and time are invested mainly in the tangible and material. One's hope for happiness is based on the size of one's bank account. Obviously, without material resources, human existence would be short lived. Who pays the rent and the food bill and the clothier? Who pays the tuition for the kids' education? How does one move about without a car? Who pays the medical bills? The list is endless and must be factored into the question. But the needs-pyramid gets to a point where there is something more needed for this elusive quality, so difficult to define, which we call happiness.

With all our money, we have widespread anxiety, distrust, loneliness, fear, and discontent. We observe something close to a terror of being alone. Why are we so often unhappy in spite of our enormously improved material status? Why is this? What does it mean? What kind of world view allows someone like Mr. Thompson to extract from a limited environment such profound feelings of contentment and fulfillment? On the other hand, how is it that someone I know who owns a $4,000,000 apartment in a very fancy building on the East Side is miserable daily? He has money, good health, a successful career, a family, and a reasonable faith level. What is he missing? Is it genetic? Or emotional? Or social? Or cultural? Or what?

Is happiness a relative thing? I recall that, years ago, the advertising industry used to attempt to plumb such dimensions. How frequently we were bombarded with those eye-catching slogans: "Happiness is a Kent cigarette" or "Happiness is owning a puppy dog" or "Happiness is owning a house in the Hamptons."

Clearly, happiness has a large subjective dimension in its makeup. What pleases me can be another man's poison. Is it merely another Rorschach test? Nonetheless, a common variable in this search must be contentment which is a pervasive feeling that the hand I have been dealt can be fulfilling, valuable and generally worthwhile. I recall one of my professors in graduate school telling us how he looked into the mirror each morning, reviewed his assets like health, love, a fulfilling job, friends, a sense of humor, a lively faith and life, itself, and said to himself: "Not bad." This is not character dwarfism but the very contrary. The more one appreciates what one has, the more one appreciates life—and gains even more. This does not lead to smugness, stagnation or indifference but, paradoxically, to personal growth. It leads to the freedom of looking around and seeing what is there.

It is ironic that the more one sees and appreciates the specific values and goods of life, the more such an emotional treasury expands. It is remarkable that sometimes we cannot recognize the happiness potential right under our noses. Experience endlessly teaches that the grass is not always greener on the other side of the fence. It hardly ever is.

Where does all this lead? One startling conclusion is that negative factors in life and contentment (even positive resignation), can make surprisingly congenial bedfellows. It depends on how one views life. At the same time, it is interesting that Jesus never promised happiness in this life. He did clearly promise something called shalom. This is a profound inner experience of order. Of tranquility. Of oughtness. But it differs from happiness which is obviously so difficult to define. Permanent happiness belongs to paradise, the state of heaven, but the deep interior feeling that things are the way they are supposed to be is attainable in this valley of tears. But how?

I suggest that the earthly happiness-peace-contentment constellation would include the following:

1. Living in the present or one day at a time. Remorse, regret and guilt are often a waste of energy. I can control my now but not my past or my future.

2. Cultivating a habit of gratitude for the blessings and joys in my immediate cosmos. Constantly recalling the street wisdom of the half-filled glass.

3. Noticing what goes on in my world. Cultivating the habit of seeing the many good things under my very nose. Becoming aware of the phoniness of the beautiful-people hoopla. Seeing that the glitz of the media is largely superficial and consequently discovering freedom from envy.

4. Instantly halting the first inklings of self-pity realizing that the pity pot is close to the most damaging human emotion.

5. Cutting the roots of the silliness of perfectionism, again realizing that the notion of perfection is an illusion which discourages real attempts at human growth.

6. Getting deeply rooted in God and His truth whereby one finally discovers one's own value as the Lord's own child. Understanding, consequently, that life is meant to be enjoyed

and that having appropriate fun is not only permitted by the Lord but is highly encouraged. This is highly linked to an authentic religious way of life which brings that profound joy of the inner awareness of walking with God.

Everyone has a right and even an obligation to figure out the best way to live one's life. Of course, we can lose that which makes us happy in this life while heaven is forever. Yet, we should, it would appear, make the most of what we have in this life and get the maximum of the happiness-peace-contentment potential in our lives. May God and Our Lady direct us to lead the good and merry Christian life.

On Being Offended by Public Religious Devotion

Is it possible that, one day in the not-too-distant future, I, as a senior citizen, might be socked with a misdemeanor just for reading my prayer book (required daily prayer for priests) on a bus? My fears stem from the following. Not only did Justice Hugo Black insist, many years ago, that absolutely nothing of government money can, in any way, be used to support any religious behavior but, with presently surfacing legal insights, I, also, might be violating someone's alleged constitutional right not to be offended. Could my reading an official Catholic and quasi-public prayer on a bus which is supported significantly by government money, become cause for an ACLU protest? Could I be arrested because I might offend a fellow passenger with my very visible personal devotion in addition to, allegedly, violating our cherished separation of state and church? One notes the word church is accurately used, if one understands history and law. But there is no separation between state and religion. The distinction is significant and substantive. My arrest would arise from an inaccurate understanding of constitutional law.

However, is there any reality to my vague discomfort that someday I might be forbidden to wear a clerical collar in the public square? Or that religious sisters could be arrested for appearing in their religious habits? Is my historical awareness (and dis-ease) of the early 20th century Mexican situation inappropriate?

Is it paranoid to imagine that someday in a wild, wide-eyed crusade reminiscent of the Salem witch hunts, crosses would be declared unlawful if visible from public streets? Is it utterly absurd to worry that I might be forbidden someday to proclaim my deepest faith beliefs by which I run my life? Even from my own pulpit? That some small-town merchant in western Canada was fined for not supporting certain homosexual causes or that an Anglican pastor in England was threatened with the loss of his parish should he continue to preach politically incorrect homilies, might be dismissed as isolated cases of nuttiness were it not for relatively concrete data indicating a well-organized secularist movement (if small in number) and one which gives me great concern.

Why my discomfort about the threat to remove the motto, "In God we trust," on our currency which has meant so much to me ever since I could read? Might we lose it? Might the courts and legislatures vote that prayer invoking the protection and guidance of God be forbidden? Could all religious symbols be removed from public buildings? If I am a chaplain in the Armed Forces, will I be forbidden to wear a cross on my uniform lapel? Will I be instructed to disguise my status as a priest and will I be designated as some kind of secular morale officer to run bingo games? Will it be forbidden to me to celebrate Holy Mass for young Catholic soldiers in a tent purchased by taxpayers' money? Will crosses be removed from the tombstones at Arlington cemetery? Will our maintenance (even if limited) of the Omaha beach cemetery shrine be neglected because so many crosses mark the graves of thousands of brave American dead who fought for our freedom and way of life? The deduction of such conclusions from certain questionable premises might well lead to the implementation of what I consider the ungodly, the un-American and the toxic. It is possible!

To counter the knee-jerk response of some of my good but naïve friends who suggest, even kindly, that I am on the verge of going bananas, I offer some reasons for my discomfort. First, the relatively recent Supreme Court decision on the sodomy laws of Texas. When Justice Scalia wrote that the majority decision well might usher in a whole series of moral breakdowns, including so-called gay marriage, one of his well-intentioned colleagues opined that such a fear was utterly unfounded, particularly the issue of same-sex marriage which was considered totally impossible.

In less than one year, the drums began to beat for marriage of same-sex partners, not merely some kind of civil recognition but specifically for marriage. Of course, no one thought that such legitimization would be acceptable to this nation. Suddenly, it is front and center. And now, to oppose or even question the prudence of legalizing, as marriage, homosexual lifestyles (considered by a majority of Americans to be destructive and immoral) is to invite such vitriol rarely even whispered in this country. There is little room for calm, adult dialogue. The notion of hearing the other guy out seems to be vanishing. As an example, we have seen the brutal shouting down of Ann Coulter who was invited to give a traditional and now controversial point of view in an American University. The intolerant treatment was unbelievable in a society presumed to be open to an exchange of ideas.

Additionally, I note the instance of Pepsi Cola's silent move to remove "Under God" from the Pledge of Allegiance which is printed on the company's soda containers (lest someone be offended). I note the move in California to remove crosses along the road because they annoy an atheist motorist. I note (as quoted by Roger Hitchcock on the Limbaugh program) that a state governor has forbidden any public prayer to end, "In Jesus' Name." I note the innumerable school principals who forbid students from voluntary (even silent) prayer before sports events and who utterly exclude any kind of religious acknowledgement at graduations. The rationale for such oppression is that someone might be offended. I note the really nutty prohibition of certain colors (red and green) in public schools at Christmas time because of a possible link to Christ which again might hurt someone's feelings. Who is the offended "someone"? Not only is he statistically minuscule but, apart from a few noisy ones, he is often shadowy and elusive. Nevertheless, whence this creeping slippery slope?

Clearly, it is a given that all Americans are guaranteed the right to freely exercise their various religions however they please. The First Amendment specifically intends to protect citizens' religious expression from government interference. Constitutionally and historically, there is no notion of protection of government from religious forces. It is simply stated that there will be no federal or national church. There is no separation of state from religion but only separation from an official church as was the case in England which strongly affected the Framers.

By an ironic legal twist, the unthinkables, noted above, somehow have become possible. In an atmosphere of "one flew over the cuckoo's nest," all the above (and much more) are gaining legal shape and form. Now to justify these un-American behaviors, someone has come up with the battle cry of absurdity: "The right not to be offended." How far does this go? Where did all this come from?

A highly respected Constitutional lawyer, Marc Levin gives a probable genesis of the tragedy in his book *Men in Black* (Regnery Publishing 2005). On page forty-eight, he references the 1962 Supreme Court ruling of *Engel v. Vitale* which outlawed state-sponsored prayer in a controversial and dubious decision which was at odds with American history. Justice A. Kennedy wrote that public benedictions were unfair pressures on un-believers to maintain respectful silence and which made them feel as outsiders. This was called the "coercion test." The implications of Kennedy's write-up are enormously dangerous to religious freedom.

Meanwhile, Professor Vincent Munoz, an American Enterprise scholar, picks this absurdity apart. He points out that the test secures "the right not to feel uncomfortable."

Such discomfort will trump (in the logic of the Court) the First Amendment's free exercise of religion. It is now beginning to apply to the right not to be offended. But does this apply to my feeling offended when each summer a "gay" parade prances down a major street in my city, holding up traffic, littering the streets, costing my city tax money to hire police for overtime pay, when they flaunt what my own faith holds to be immodest, when they shout obscenities about my religious leader? Apparently, this is different because they tell me that their behavior is only establishing identity while people like me are breaking the tenets of the First Amendment when we publicly pray a general and silent prayer or even mention a deity.

In effect, where does the right not to be offended stop? Is there a limit which reasonable people can agree upon? Or who decides what is offensive? Further, what happens to the concept of democracy which, in my understanding, is the rule of the will of majority? Is a country to be ruled by a vocal and committed tiny minority? I thought this was a discarded, pre-Christian and obsolete form of rule called oligarchy.

Americans are rightly proud of our history and our political system, the like of which has never been seen anywhere in the history of man. It is important to remember that the Declaration of Independence (an authentic clue as to the intentions of the Founders) is not merely an historical document. It explicitly recognizes that human rights do not derive from kings or parliaments, government or the judiciary. It states that rights come from God. "Endowed by their Creator with certain unalienable rights…." Our religious practice is not alien to our political philosophy but even integral to it. It is obvious that the fears expressed above are real. They must be countered since the material of the fears is basically an attack on our founding principles. Our tradition teaches that we do not rely on government (and certainly not the courts) as the source of our rights. An elementary sophistication about the source of our rights which are unalienable quickly indicates a source higher than our selves. If such rights came, not from a higher source, but from the state, they become malleable and are therefore not unalienable. Even a dirty-necked kid from the tenements like me can see that this is a prescription for tyranny against which our forefathers fought a terrible war. Marc Levin taught me this. He is clearly right. May God protect these United States!

Hating, Loving and Creative Thinking are Largely Learned (like almost everything else)

The Feast of the Conversion of St. Paul on January 25th, 2006

How did it come to be that I, a half Jew, am a passionate follower of Jesus the Christ while my Jewish cousins who share much of my gene legacy, passionately do not? I resemble them in my facial features. I talk in a similar fashion as do they. We laugh at the same jokes. We all enjoy a spirited debate. We all rage at the Holocaust. We all fiercely believe in education. We are all high energy people. Most of them are smarter than I am. And certainly better looking. So, I pose to myself some knotty questions on this Catholic feast day which celebrates the spiritual reversal of a short, bandy-legged, bald-headed, frenetic, enthusiastic little Jew from extreme hostility towards the crucified Galilean to an almost fanatic devotion to Him.

How come that I am a Catholic believer and my cousins are not? How do I explain to myself with any kind of honesty why I am so blessed with this pearl of great price and they are not? While I fully believe in the reverential and grateful Catholic position that all faith is an unearned gift from God the Father, I am strangely fixated on the theological principle that God's glorious grace builds on nature. Of course, I am bursting with what I think is mature pride in my Church. I am convinced that the Catholic manner of life is a splendid way to live. I am delighted that I am a Catholic. Nevertheless, I have questions. Questions of nature. Questions of culture. Questions of environment. I wonder and I muse what effect these factors have on human personality and functioning?

My own studies of human behavior, both past and present, shout out (at least to me) certain pre-articulate and intuitive potentials of our human condition. I remember the insights of a subhuman human (A. Hitler) who saw that very young human beings can be molded into brutal, dedicated followers if skillful learning manipulations are used. He understood the plasticity of the human psyche whereby values might be learned to fit his personal criteria.

Obviously, this insight can have a positive side, again depending upon one's view of what positive means. We have probably all heard of the alleged Jesuit educational principle, "Give me the child early enough and I will turn him into anything you wish!" Shades of J.B. Watson, the founder of American Behaviorism. And it is all about learning. School boys learn of Pavlov's drooling dog whereby instinctive processes of survival (such as eating) become the baseline for manipulating behavior by linking an automatic response with a planned stimulus.

And certainly, studies in human development testify to the incredibly quick learning that goes on in the life even of a newborn infant. My sense is that such knowledge can be applied to religious faith whereby the child is given a reasonable life platform, upon which to build a life of morality and ethics. The research psychologist, B.F. Skinner, for all his sometimes-nutty convictions, did clarify for us the now widely accepted behavior modification system. Reward the acceptable behavior and it will increase. Withhold the reward and the unacceptable behavior will tend to decrease. A nod here, a smile there, an attentive posture, all can subtly modify behavior. We are not chimps to be manipulated but we are vulnerable to micro rewards or lack of them. With some modifications to his, sometimes complex, Modification Theory, we might use his insights in our attempts to understand and elevate human behavior.

However, it is elementary that certain human behaviors are innate and unlearned, such as breathing, eating, being sexually attracted to another, suckling at mother's breast, pulling away from painful stimuli, raising one's hand in defense against an approaching blow. Constitutionally, we are designed to survive which is perhaps the first law of human nature. Yet many micro behaviors are learned so as to function on a dimension beyond the biologic and the physiologic—even if nudged along by nature's plan.

This is the more subtle dimension which interests me. Values, goals, purposes, love levels, sacred honor, and virtue differ substantially, often from one person to another. This is the area of learning which we ponder. I personally believe that the Lord imprinted in all human hearts a basic sense of right and wrong, roughly analogous to the Ten Commandments. Yet, I also believe that this basic imprint can be almost muted by human psychological and cultural factors. Retardation of the moral sense (as well as the esthetic) is understandable in terms of a primitive and deprived environment. Kohlberg's extensive studies decades ago illustrated this point in his work on the multi levels of moral development. Of course, in the cognitive realm, we know real cases of organically wounded children who have truly serious learning difficulties. While this statistically minimal is of concern, the larger picture investigated here is about learned behavior which could be moral or ethical or cognitive.

I was privileged to interview the articulate William F. Buckley on my own television show many years ago. He spoke of the stimulating and elevated dinner conversation that happened each night in his home. This climate so stimulated him that somewhere around the age of five, he wrote an angry letter to King George of England demanding that the English repay the United States war debts from World War I. This differs significantly from my own early experience where the usual table silence was occasionally broken by something like "pass da salt." Can I speculate that the confidence of Bill Buckley as compared with my own shyness and tentativeness might, in part, be traced to environment? Did we both learn from our surroundings—even if we didn't know we were learning verbal behavior? Did we imitate what was vibed to us from our special world?

I have listened to recordings of my father's voice, noted his vocal modulation, his phrasing, pronunciation and pitch, then listened to recordings of my own voice and found a startling similarity. Did I not learn my speech patterns which were neither inborn nor unlearned? I did not come to this world as a complete, factory tested package. I learned almost everything of my early life from environment.

In South Africa I lived for years under an iniquitous system called Apartheid. It was a truism there that little children, aged three or four would play joyously with each other even if one were Zulu and the other White (or European) with no awareness of skin differences. By the time they became seven or eight, their behavior changed. No longer un-self-conscious pals but now *baas* (boss) and servant. Their mode of social interaction drastically changed. Why? How? What happened in those intervening years to make such a profound and drastic change in a human relationship?

The children learned, even without knowing they were learning, that their society disapproved of their intimacy. There were pervasive, racial norms which were verbal, non-verbal and demanding. People learned to behave in a clearly un-Christian manner because of the enormous power held by society to approve or disapprove.

Isn't this true, in some way, of language, mores, cultures? For example, in the United States kids learn to love playing baseball, the national sport which is regarded in South Africa as quaint and tacky. In Johannesburg and Cape Town we play a sport of good manners and sophistication. It is called cricket and played leisurely in spotlessly white trousers while spectators sip hot tea under shady trees. That is what the South African environment teaches and what citizens learn.

A priest client of mine was told by a religious person when he was in the sixth grade that he could never be a priest. He was too stupid, she said. He could never pass the exams and handle the intricacies of the clerical life. On top of a dysfunctional family background, he carried this punishing inner voice within him for years as he struggled with the belief that others viewed him as inadequate, impotent and ineffectual. Since authority (his environment) told him, he learned to view himself thusly. This self-destructive learned self-image hampered him all his life even though he did become a priest and subsequently earn two master's degrees which he personally discounted as just due to hard work and good luck. In fact, he was not born that way, i.e., to disesteem himself. He was unknowingly taught to be that way.

My friend and psychiatrist colleague, Dr. Arnie Zucker, delights in singing into the ears of his one-year-old grandsons some traditional Jewish ditties which generally carry the following theme. "Aren't you glad you are a circumcised little Jewish boy and that you weren't born a goy?" He clearly understands, as do I approvingly, that little human beings are taught from the earliest moments of life how they will live. With constant approvals like this, these little boys will grow up to be clearly defined in their Jewish identities. This is not being defined by hormones and genes.

Sexual orientation is a factor of great relevance here. Persons who suffer from same-sex attraction (SSA) sometimes, in what I believe is an ultimately ineffectual attempt to relieve their undoubted suffering, will insist that they were born that way, i.e., homosexual. Often parents, in their own attempt for guilt relief, will insist that there must be some sort of biologic basis for their children's homosexuality. To believe that a parent might have unconsciously contributed to such an unhappy orientation would be an enormously heavy burden to carry. The deduction from the being-born-that-way belief is that the Lord Himself clearly ordained that some of His children should have a sexual life with persons of the same sex. There would then be no guilt. No social shame. All would be paradisiacal. Ironically, lobbyists for such a view battle fiercely, using learning theory to achieve their goal of glorifying a false identity. Such a false identity would demand the following stance. The clear teachings of Scripture would have to be denied as would the teachings of the Judeo-Christian world along with the sad lessons of homosexual history.

In the absence of any serious scientific data supporting biologic basis for homosexuality, the available voluminous correlation studies become significant. One notable example is the factor of defensive detachment with male homosexuals. This means that a very young male perceives (possibly inaccurately) rejection from his father figure who is physically distant or abusive, undemonstrative, unloving in action in words, and uninterested. The young one feels rejected or uncomfortable and pre-empts parental (or surrogate) rejections by detaching himself from his father and he does the rejecting before he is rejected. He has learned to defend himself from a (perceived) projected painful experience. But for the rest of his life he will be seeking healing as he searches, even unconsciously, for the love of his father. I know that this is only one of the many learning factors associated with the drab parameters of the "gay" life. In my own clinical work stretching over thirty years, such detachment has been, not exclusively, but very frequently operational. In the research studies it is paramount.

However, this one piece of data can be invaluable for young fathers who might not understand the urgency of showing affection to their very young sons. (Obviously, we have concern for female children who have a somewhat different psychic structure).

Granting the constitutional fund of libido which is obviously innate (and planned so by the Creator/Designer), we can learn how to direct and channel the enormous power of sex into the great plan. It is intellectually (not emotionally) simple, as Pope Benedict XVI pointed out in his encyclical on love, *Deus caritas est* (*God is Love*), that sexual love belongs only to the union of a man and a woman in a monogamous committed relationship called marriage. The sexual freedom so cherished by modern liberals, leads to bad eros and broken hearts. A bad environment teaches how to ruin one's life. Conversely, one can learn to love as a responsible adult presuming a healthy personal environment. We have seen such love flourish within the Courage movement almost endlessly.

Of course, there is always a sexual drive from the human physical constitution which is ever tempting, ever conflicting and so interestingly called the "id" by Freud. Fortunately, one learns that, with the help of God, one can live with integrity and virtue. We can put the lid on the id!

Research Science tells us that the human being's learning potential is unimaginable, so vast is its depth. It would be a pity if we give up too soon on the troubled or limited human being through our own indolence or ignorance. Bad learning can often and surprisingly be unlearned with real promise of re-learning the helpful and the good. Young parents would be far ahead of the game if they would apply principles of learning (not necessarily from books) to babies. We remember that little children are imitators of the heroes of their lives, principally their parents. Certainly, there are several inborn obvious factors as noted above but there are treasures in the child which may never be surfaced, unless knowledgeable and clearly identified people are present. And childhood years are crucial. This is more than learning soccer or ballet. This is learning how to be a healthy person. Is this nature or nurture? Who really knows? Both are present. But we cannot ignore the environment and its effect on loving and hating and thinking creatively.

Nor can we ignore the environmental matrix as the ground for the great gift of faith. How did I get my faith? Certainly, from the Lord but with the help of believing and simple Catholics. Perhaps, my Jewish cousins would be saying the rosary today and marching for life if they had had the social advantages I had. The Catholic Church prods us to recall that, after all, grace builds on nature. While God's grace clearly abounds, we are expected to do our part. In this great mystery of searching for God, we are all teachers as well as learners. May the loving and merciful be God be with us!

What Does It Mean To Be A Priest? (An Answer of an Eighty-Three-Year-Old Priest)

I was ordained a Catholic priest on May 1, 1948 by a tall, gray haired, distinguished, stately bishop who instructed me and my classmates about the state we had just entered. But what was that state of priest? What did it mean? What had happened to me?

That very day, a young Paulist priest, about six years into the priesthood and whom I viewed as an older chap, casually remarked to me that I would spend the rest of my life trying to figure out what did happen to me. Now, with my typical late-reaction tendency after fifty-six years of "priesting," I begin to plumb even further what he implied. And with some apprehension, I have a sense of the unsettling priest insight of "Take back Thy Power." And it slightly frightens me. But what power? Let me muse on power in the priesthood.

In 1946, a Russian woman, Baroness Catherine de Hueck or Mrs. Eddie Doherty, addressed over 400 seminarians, all of us preparing for the Catholic priesthood at the Catholic University in Washington, D.C. She was a woman of remarkable charisma who emanated the very essence of a mysterious power. She vibed out an energy which permeated the huge hall. She spoke with remarkable vigor of her work in establishing centers for the hurting poor, the dirty poor, unwanted and rejected by clean citizens. She had gotten in there and had hurled herself into the sad and grim world of poverty. We were almost dumbstruck with her emotionality.

Yet, as impressive as her observations were to us about our duty to engage in the social needs of our age, she utterly bowled us over with her view of priest. She urged, pleaded, cajoled us to remember that, once we were ordained priests, to "walk among the people, and you will strew blessings along your way." She didn't urge that we should be great scholars or preachers or fund raisers or policy makers. She said: "Just walk among the people. Walk among the people." What was her meaning?

That was so, so long ago and it has rung in my heart down through all these years. I can still hear her proclaiming that admonition. It has been an integral part of my own spirituality and identity. In that statement is contained, I think, the core of what a priest is. In there is the profound reality of what really did happen to me that joyful day as I knelt before Bishop Stephen Donahue.

When I was a little kid in St. Paul the Apostle grammar school in New York City, the Holy Cross Sisters taught us something about a seal or character of Baptism. It was as if God had stamped the soul with a mark whereby the lucky one was adopted by the Lord in a very special way. Once one was sealed, it was forever. We intuited by a pre-articulation that there was no way one could be unbaptized. No matter what kind of child of God I became, good or bad or ugly or nice, I would always have that divine Father for eternity. I would carry that seal or mark with me wherever I would go, wherever I should walk. Whatever I would do, consciously or not, I would make my way marked for God. Were I to rant later in my life and resign from that priesthood, my membership would remain intact despite any personal rebellion or sin. My resignation would be inoperative. I would simply be an inactive, non-practicing child of my heavenly Father.

There was a power in this marking (or as Sister called it, "character"). My prayers, my actions, my thoughts, my feelings were all suffused with this foundational level of being. We were also taught that there was an advanced state of such being in a sacrament named Confirmation where we would be more deeply marked by the Holy Spirit and gifted with fortitude whereby we would be prepared to endure and suffer and even fight for the ancient faith. All this by a power from elsewhere which we believed to be from the Lord. Now it was to be no longer I but the Lord working through me in my day-to-day Christian life. I carried these markings with me everywhere I went. Conscious awareness was not necessarily called for; it just was!

Living in such a framework made it easy for me to move into the towering world of the priesthood. We were taught (and I deeply believe it) that through the Sacrament of Holy Orders we were profoundly marked a third and final time (and this is the point) as *alter Christus*, or other Christ! From henceforth, we would be empowered to act in the very person of Jesus, Himself.

This would mean that I, a dirty necked kid from Manhattan's tenements, would, through the priesthood of Jesus, take bread and wine and transform such into the body and blood of the Lord! This profound marking would be with me and in me, as a very part of my essence, for eternity. Whether I became another Iscariot or another Xavier, I would be priest forever. And, further, I would be a priest whether I was conscious of it or not. We were constantly reminded of the Scriptural point: You are a priest forever according to the order of Melchizedek, not according to Luther or Bing Crosby or Joe DiMaggio.

Graham Greene portrayed the insight marvelously well in his engrossing novel, *The Power And The Glory*, in which he describes a bad priest, a drunkard, a lecher, an exploiter of the poor but who, through the power of the priesthood can and does celebrate the sacrifice of the Mass for the Catholic faithful.

They personally know his faults but they also know his ghostly powers. In effect, it is again not I but "Him Who strengthens me." This is why even a proud priest has to be humble at the consecration of the Mass when the transubstantiation occurs! He knows that it is not he who does this miracle every day; he acts only *in persona Christi*.

With an insight that the Catholic laity has owned for centuries, the priest is treated with incredible respect even with all the scandals of recent years. It is certainly not because of the human side of these men, but because of the Alter Christus understanding.

The Knights of Columbus of the third degree have a special commitment to protect and enhance the Catholic priesthood. Many Catholics still respectfully open doors for priests, give them seats of honor, call them father and seek counsel and guidance from them, despite the smearing and cheapening of the office by some unworthy clerics. And why? Because of the mark, the quasi-metaphysical branding of this priest soul. The Christ is present in this vessel of clay in a way nowhere else to be found. This is all about the presence of Jesus.

This is also a huge unreachable feeling about Christ. It was almost humorous that during the filming of Mel Gibson's masterpiece, *The Passion of The Christ*, some of the workers on the set, moved by the sight of the actor Jim Caviezel (thirty-three-years old with initials J.C.), made up as the Redeemer, would kneel as he passed by. They were so deeply into the passion of Jesus that they were impelled to reverence the Master, even though it was only a very good man taking the role.

This clearly surfaces the erroneous notion that the priest should be one of the boys. Perhaps, painfully, the priest realizes that he is set apart and that he one of God's special ones. He can never be like one of the guys and be true to his calling. He might use Marine language. He might hang out in bars. He might engage in whoring. He might get seduced by money. No matter what, he is set apart. Such a realization has become such a burden for some priests that they have left the priesthood to get out from under the guilt of being another Christ.

To be a priest with this understanding that I am another Christ and that I cannot have the consolations of other men and that I am set apart, means a huge loneliness in my life. It means that I, like Jesus also must have my personal Gethsemane.

So, to set a man into the priesthood without his understanding the mark of the Lord on him and the terrible price that he must pay for his privilege of being Christ in the world would be cruelty personified. I recall a young priest who left and returned to his former life, telling me that in the Seminary he was in graduate school and not in formation to be a priest. It was as if he were preparing for dentistry or journalism or public relations. Another young priest who likewise returned to his secular life mocked the notion of seal and testified that he never heard the poof of the Holy Spirit marking him as priest. Without an identity of *alter Christus*, the priest is severely hampered in his personal growth and happiness.

The poor judgment of seminary personnel and/or their theological shallowness has allowed such young men to think of priesthood as a job or profession or social engineer. The harm done these students is incalculable. Obviously, we are beginning to reap the unhappy effects of the poor leadership and training of recent decades. Clearly, the priest's power stems from his being set aside by the marking of Ordination. Obviously, again, the greatest expression of this power is the Mass where he offers God back to God in the most perfect worship possible to man. As correct as is the notion of meal at the Mass, sacrifice is more theologically central to our meaning. Emphasizing the eating as paramount can feed into a more humanistic or even narcissistic notion of worship.

The great Fr. James Gillis CSP, reminded me as a young priest that a priest who does not offer sacrifice is a misnomer. Priest instantly implies offering a sacrifice. I am enthused when I hear the beautiful Gospel hymn "Were You There (When They Crucified My Lord)?" because I can almost shout: yes, yes, yes I am there every day when they crucify Him because I offer the Holy Sacrifice of the Mass which re-presents Calvary for me.

I am appalled and saddened when I learn that some modern priests will not say Mass unless they have to. Does such a priest not know who he is? That when he says Mass, Jesus moves in him as in no one else? Does he know that when he gives absolution He forgives the sins of man in the person of Christ? That at that moment in one sense he is Christ? I doubt this unenthusiastic priest knows who he is. I doubt that he sees his own identity as a priest.

I tried to make the point with a woman Eucharistic minister in a nursing home who told me of the many confidences she received from the residents.

If I could only hear confessions, she said, I could be of such help. I suggested that she could hear as many confessions as she liked. There is, however, an essential point to be noted. She couldn't absolve them from sin. Only Christ can do that and Christ does it through His priests. Only they are so marked and empowered.

So, when a priest is overcome with what he is and he cries out in a spiritual terror: "Take back Thy power," one can appreciate this man feeling inadequate even if so honored. And always in his deepest self, he knows that others of his culture were more worthy and smarter and more sensible and braver and better looking and endlessly better suited than he. But always he knows that it is not a question of choosing but of being chosen.

Finally, the Russian was right. Let the priest simply walk among the people. Let the Christ blessings be strewn along the way. When the priest walks, Christ walks in a special way in him because of the marking. This is Christ's man and if one looks deeply enough with faith and some theological sophistication, this is Christ.

Weak Catholic Religious Education: How it Affects Faith

In 1936, the Feast of Our Lady of Lourdes, February 11th was a momentous day for devout Catholics. The apparition of the Mother of God at Lourdes to a simple peasant French girl was celebrated de rigueur in the uncomplicated household I called my home. For nine mornings and evenings, a novena, we devoted ourselves to this powerful celestial protector called Our Lady of Lourdes. Under the strong will of my Irish Grandmother and the sweet but unyielding direction of the Holy Cross Sisters, all of us (except for my Jewish father), dutifully attended Mass each morning and services at night where we heard stirring sermons on God's power and His desire to gift us, provided we asked Him through the great lady we called Our Blessed Mother.

We made our petitions which ranged from requesting good health or a steady job to finding my beloved lost dog, Mickey Finn. We lit candles with a little prayer. After waiting on long lines, we went to confession, received absolution from our sins and resolved to amend our sinful ways. We dropped our nickel or dime in the poor box and felt very good about ourselves. We felt kinder to our fellow human beings, lied less and helped to clean up after dinner.

The huge Paulist Church was literally packed each Novena night. Unless one came reasonably early, standing room was the only option. The side chapels were crammed with folding chairs. The men sat on red pillows placed on the steps leading up to the great sanctuary where we would witness the benediction of the Most Blessed Sacrament at the conclusion of each evening ceremony. Faith was rampant. The grace of Jesus fell like rain. Out of such a socio-religious matrix came the

Greatest Generation, those who survived the Great Depression and the suffering of World War II.

Within such a matrix, however, it was easy to be actively religious. It was easy to incorporate one's spiritual beliefs into daily life. But it was taken for granted that there was something to incorporate. Our meaningful spiritual life presupposed a whole structure of religious doctrine which we, as children, year after year, learned daily from religious sisters. These nuns had a special kind of infallibility which was, "Sister sez...," beyond which there could be no question. Sister told us we would have a serious obligation to worship God each Sunday through the Holy Mass. We would receive Jesus in Holy Communion, not as a symbol but the Lord Himself. We could have our sins forgiven through the sacrament of Penance. We would have reasonable certainty about the truths of the faith through the leadership of the Pope, the Vicar of Jesus Christ on earth and the successor to Peter the Rock.

We could pray to a dazzling array of saints who were scholars, doctors, soldiers, beggars, married, single, rich, poor, Japanese, Irish, African and American—all ready to help us in times of grief, fear or puzzlement. The sisters taught us to aspire ourselves to such spiritual heights and to believe that it is possible for us, too, aided by the grace of the Lord we worshipped. Life made sense while we acknowledged absurdity and weakness. The large answers were clear even if the crosses remained difficult and painful. Catholicism for us was more than a Creed or philosophy. It was a pervasive way of Life. Affectively, we were close to God.

Unless one has been living in the Gobi Desert for fifty years it is obvious that there has been a change in the Catholic way of life. On Feb. 11, 2006, seventy years later, there was hardly a mention of Our Lady of Lourdes. Today the great Paulist Church is hardly ever packed to the doors. There is merely a sprinkling of communicants. There are no more Holy Cross Sisters to open the young souls to the glories of the faith. There is open and sometimes heretical dissent from the core teachings of the faith. Nearly one third of Catholics don't believe in the Real Presence of Christ in the Eucharist. Unbelievably, some priests doubt the truth of transubstantiation, alleging that community building is more important than faith. Visits to the Blessed Sacrament are rare. Making the Stations of the Cross as a devotion is a quaint anachronism. To see some adult making his beads (saying his Rosary), even in the case of religious, might raise some progressive eyebrows. Catholic leaders, including popes, are categorized and dismissed as Neanderthal, former young Nazis or mere Italian bureaucrats.

Few Catholics go to confession. Many believe it doesn't really matter what religion one professes. Some Catholics support abortion programs believing one's immediate conscience trumps revealed truth. Many Catholics support same-sex marriages while others practice homosexual behavior with a mindset justifying illicit sexual pleasures. And of course, these persons often blatantly announce that—yes, they are Catholics who go to church often, have their children baptized or married in the Catholic manner and send in an occasional check for charity. They apparently see no disconnect between their personal lives and the abstract Catholicism they murkily profess. This is, at times, publicly manifested in the cases of Catholic politicians who bristle whenever bishops challenge them in the public forum.

What happened? Of course, there are many possible variables which have contributed to this sad state. The possible list is long. I suggest that one measurable variable which has fed into the decay is very weak religious instruction. But one suspects that many modern Catholics don't even know what traditional religious instruction means. In their traditional ability to joke about their own weaknesses, my Jewish family told me this relevant story. A rich Jewish entrepreneur wishes to have his new Jaguar blessed. He approaches an Orthodox rabbi for the blessing who asks innocently: "What's a Jaguar?" A Conservative rabbi similarly responds: "What's a Jaguar?" But a hot shot/modern Reform Rabbi responds: "What's a Blessing?"

Many modern Catholics will innocently wonder, "what's traditional religious instruction?" They usually lack the warm flexibility and confidence of the Jewish soul which has been refined in the furnace of bigotry and hatred. The Jew learned to laugh at himself in his quest for survival, seen tragically in the example of the Russian and Polish shtetls. Not so with the modern sad Catholic, who might, in fact, be in objective heresy or schism. He is defensive and dour. His anger and depression are getting more widespread. A psychologist might wonder whether we are witnessing a colossal unconscious adolescent rebellion against a parental figure.

Some years ago, a columnist of the liberal *National Catholic Reporter*, himself the recipient of the riches of Catholic tradition, nostalgically pined for the glory of his religious youth. He watched the so-called religious education of his children with dismay, where the dominant instruction core was not the Eucharist or grace or prayer or Lourdes but rather an elusive goal of self-esteem.

Under the influence of so many Catholic educators, some of whom I met in my own graduate psychology work, the religious education programs focused on feeling good about yourself. It was implied that a warm navel gazing stance would be more helpful for happiness than an awareness of life's purpose and the means of reaching eternal happiness with God and inner peace in this life.

This columnist wrote of the Catholicism of his youth which was taught like a gorilla triumphantly thumping his chest. He compared this past glory with the present state of religious instruction which features rills and rocks, running streams, sheaves of wheat flowing in the wind, quasi-animism and which, effectively, focuses, not on God, the Lord and Master, but on the self. The result is an uninformed, pallid, pale religious pablum.

Such an enormous disservice to the Catholic people is staggering. And the weakness is not confined to the laity alone. The *New Oxford Review* (April 1997) challenged a Catholic bishop of Colorado who announced that he would never, in the future, preach against any kind of sin from the pulpit, lest someone might be offended! To speak of abortion or homosexual acting out for him is now out of bounds. He can't challenge any sin because it might damage someone's self-esteem. The sinner might feel rejected or guilty. He is saturated with the new Catholicism but alas, what happens to those who look to him for guidance? Where is the call to repentance? Where is the awareness of the cross so deep in the faith and devotion of 1936?

We thank God for teachers like Bishop Fabian of Nebraska who will not be silent about sin. Thank the Lord for Dr. James Dobson and Billy Graham and C.S. Lewis who teach the deep truths of God. The Catholics of 1936 were raised on the simple *Baltimore Catechism* and have been condemned ever since as being underdeveloped and rigid. In spite of actual limitations of such a religious formation, Catholics of that time knew something of their faith and they acted on it. By comparison with today's disorientation and desert wandering, 1936 looks pretty good.

Will we ever see the vigorous, enthusiastic faith of my youth? Oh, yes, but not in our time since it will take a generation to erase the excesses and mistakes of the recent past. We need real teachers who, truly informed, are not afraid to speak God's truth. We need real people who value goodness above popularity. May Our Lady of Lourdes protect us.

Hypocrisy and Religion

My cardiologist is a very decent sort of chap, even when he is thumping away at my aorta, pushing on my left ventricle and bellowing, "Breathe through your mouth." However, my last exam became a role reversal situation when he startled me by revealing a disillusionment at his brother's departure from a religious order. Confused as I was, I felt that somehow I was expected to minister to my physician minister. But what does one say to offer consolation or even a word of explanation on religious severance after fifteen years of presumably devoted, sincere service to the Lord's people?

The ex-religious explained his departure by his perception of unbearable hypocrisy[10] of the religious whose community life he shared. He seemed surprised to discover that people in religion are just as selfish, lazy, manipulative and phony as the average fellow who works as a Wall Street trader or the lady who sells hats at Bergdorf Goodman. I, myself, have lived for sixty-four years in religious community, given countless retreats and lectures to clergy and religious and have found similar human behaviors but that is only half the story.

How did he miss the abundant generosity, kindness and friendliness that pervades most religious communities—even today when widespread secular narcissism has seeped into God's own acre? Did he not meet the broken person striving for holiness who, contritely, makes amends after being sarcastic or cold to a fellow religious? Did he not see the day-by-day attempts at prayer in the midst of very busy and demanding service to others? Did he not see these vessels of clay wrestling with their God to make sense out of much of the nonsense of their lives? Did he never hear the testimony of saints, such as John Berchmanns who painfully admitted that religious community life is a purgatory? A purgatory which highlights and magnifies human failings as well as human splendor? Of course, selective friendships and greetings are rampant as are hurts and slights and even un-Christian shunning. I once lived with a fellow religious who had a list of people he wouldn't talk to. It was a common joke to ask another religious if he was on the list. Of course, there are innumerable instances of this kind of hypocrisy. But isn't there another side of the coin?

I am surprised that he was surprised. My assumption is that Catholic religious know and reasonably understand the basic doctrine of original sin whereby all of us, intelligent or dopey, young or old, healthy or ill, will be tempted to be proud, envious, lazy, lustful, angry, mean, avaricious and vengeful. The priest who is too busy or annoyed to meet the request of an anxious Catholic for sacramental confession is, on first impression, beneath my contempt, but I try to understand that there are unconscious and conscious dynamics working in him that are beyond my awareness. It is not for me to judge. Perhaps, in every human being, we might find weaknesses and modes of behavior that might be labeled hypocrisy.

The Catholic Church teaches that there is a fundamental incompletion in all human beings. No one escapes. Only Jesus who was God (as well as man) and His Blessed Mother (by singular theological exception) can claim true and complete integration. Even on Ash Wednesday, the Church reminds us that we are dust, and highly limited by space and time. I am surprised that a modern religious is unaware that all religious communities represent a slice of that population we call the human race. That tainted and broken human population is the pool from which come all religious vocations. Ideally, I would like my religious leaders, male and female to be perfect human beings, always loving, always, intelligent, always kind, always there for me. If I really believed that I would suspect that there is something in the water I drink.

Yet, it seems to me that some of the most terrifying words of the gentle Jesus were reserved for those whom he called hypocrites. These were the ones whom He labels "whited sepulchers," clean looking on the outside but rotten inside. It surfaces for me a recollection of the old Roman god, Janus, who had two faces to be used expediently according to the appropriate situation. Clearly, there is a difference between keeping personal secrets to oneself (a moral choice) and pretending to believe something one does not (or even pretending not to believe when one does). While there is no moral need to splatter one's total self all over the landscape, there is a vital Christian imperative to try to match one's behavior with one's stated belief.

In fact, this principle applies not only to religious people but to anyone who seriously pursues what we call the will of the Almighty, the Lord Himself. When, as reported in a New York newspaper recently, a local Rabbi cajoles women congregants to have sex with him under the guise of a Jewish ritual, he is a hypocrite. As is the Catholic priest who has sexual relationships with adolescents under the pretense of helping them to mature. He is a desperate hypocrite. Or the public high school teacher who molests his intimidated students, too fearful to resist or report him. Or any son or daughter of Adam/Eve who feigns virtue, belief or even feelings.

How many times I have heard the old saw from fallen-away Catholics that the reason for their non-practice is the hypocrisy of Catholics who attend Mass on Sundays. It is alleged that these Catholic hypocrites go only to show off their high couture or possibly to maintain a social or professional contact. While this might be true in isolated instances, particularly with politicians who pointedly carry big, highly visible Bibles, on Sunday mornings, it is insulting to the millions of good-hearted people who do attend their various denominations sincerely and with full intent of living godly lives. Who are the real hypocrites? It is fascinating to me to discover that many of the people I have encountered with that rationalization, are themselves engaging in or living with situations which are antithetical to the codes of the great religions. To attend services in temple or church might be too anxiety provoking for this critic. Attendance could mean a challenge to his laziness or his carnality or his dishonesty. To call others hypocrites becomes an excuse for him. Yet, his rationalization relieves him of a strenuous effort to please God. Those faithful persons who worship their God with dignity and silence do not need to trumpet their prayer life. They are well aware of the basic spiritual axiom: God who sees in secret, rewards in secret. Perhaps, the noisy criticism of those who are too involved with Mammon is all the reward they will get.

If believing people (of any religion) fail in their prayers or their charity or their self-control, do they repent and reform and try again? If so, then these people are truly sincere, even if they fail. The critic doesn't even try. In one of the recent Courage[11] meetings, a newcomer to the group who had broken free of the gay lifestyle, commented on the absence of self-loathing in the verbal witnessing of the members. His previous experience with SSA people, in other groups, had been rife with self-hatred and self-depreciation but the Courage people seemed pervaded with a sense of self-respect. The explanation derives from the Catholic insight of the second chance and the constant resurrection (i.e., the sacrament of Penance or Reconciliation). Coupled with the insistent Catholic teaching that all men and women are loved by God who sent His Son, Jesus, to die for all of us and our sins (translated as value of a person), the encouragement to pick oneself up and try all over again takes root in one's self-identity. Then the soul hears the message: Keep on trying. Keep up the good fight. Don't quit. You are basically good if marginally wounded. Miracles do happen.

Courage teaches its members the meaning of original sin and its illumination on human behavior. It teaches that the disciplining of the disordered tendency for same-sex can be a platform of holiness as in the Blessed Apostle Paul mode with his "thorn in the side." Even if the disorder is never removed, it can be contained by God's great grace and can allow the person to reach spiritual heights he never imagined! This is not hypocrisy. This is real virtue wherein these SSA people do not feign. They face the facts of their lives and struggle for the sake of the Lord to achieve and maintain interior chastity. Is it that the cynical critics dislike struggle or effort and prefer the instant gratification so cherished in modern culture?

Still, fakery (or hypocrisy) and not-revealing things are two different issues. Cardinal Levada, in an address to the seminarians at the North American College in Rome, recently suggested that an SSA priest would be well advised to keep his sexual ambiguity to himself. The need of some gay priests to publicize their gayness to Catholics whose interest is more in sizzling bacon and Sunday newspapers, speaks, not to the spiritual good of parishioners, but to underdeveloped psyches playing at being clergymen. Keeping one's sexual preferences to oneself could well indicate some attempt at generosity in protecting the faithful from confusion and disillusionment. To argue that such self-disclosure on a Sunday morning is necessary for the priest's own honesty is to high light the perceived priorities of the gay priest. He is interested in himself and not in the peaceful growth of God's people.

Christian spirituality necessarily involves some form of the cross which, in effect, translates into affective love of the Lord. While human failure is inevitable, in priests and peasants, laddies and lassies, and in all children of Adam, the splendor of human goodness still shines through all the muck and hypocrisy. Let us then sing the praises, under God, of being human!

On Reaching Eight-Five Years of Age!

I was born eight-five years ago today in the ground floor apartment of a New York City brownstone. It was Easter Sunday morning, at dawn. Although, the old Catholic ladies of that era thought that the sun danced on Easter morn, I was too occupied to check it out. I was grasping for the dawn in that dingy front bedroom—as the local physician, Dr. Sprague, was tugging me out of my mother's womb. My mother's (twin and older) sisters had just returned from Mass at the Paulist church and were agog with the excitement that there was a new Catholic (and half-Jewish) boy in the McArdle clan.

I would live in a circumscribed neighborhood for the immediate future, worshipping at the Paulist Church, learning the ropes of our own street (called in the local parlance "sixty foist" street) with the local dirty necks, of which I was one, attending the Paulist grammar school for eight years and occasionally risking the long trek to Central Park where we played baseball, football and watched the awesome animals in the zoo. We also liked to see a tree occasionally. We played creative street games which cost nothing for equipment or space. In our ignorance of how the other half lived, we were happy.

We were apparently poor. I was never aware of that since we always had three meals a day, had cyclically new clothes and we laughed a lot. Everyone I knew lived the same way. Occasionally some family would be evicted or thrown out on the street with all their furniture and few belongings. This never happened to me. Hence, I never gave that possibility a thought. It never struck me that because I didn't go away on vacations or that my family didn't have a car (or machine as they called it), that there was something inferior to my way of life. I lived in the present and felt very loved by all my family, especially by my Jewish father and my laughing Irish mother and my loving Grandmother. I was relatively content. It was the Great Depression era anyway. It was the era of, "Buddy can you spare a dime," and of well-dressed guys selling apples on the corner. I felt lucky or blessed but certainly secure. I just somehow knew that I would always have three squares and a flop.

That eerie sense of confidence has always stayed with me all these years. Somehow I have known I'll be OK and will always make it. More than hormones or ganglia, this sense of trust has fed my *joie de vivre* and my enthusiasm for what others have called the banal and repetitious. My prayer has been: "My God stands by me. I place all my trust in Him." I have had a great life, or more accurately a delicious one. I have experienced the profundity of the Catholic faith which has sustained and nourished me through stress and strain. The faith which clearly taught me the endless love of God the father for me, the marvelous comradeship of Jesus the Lord, the indwelling of the Holy Spirit. It has made real the affection of the Blessed Mother and the endless and dazzling array of saints I can pray to.

I have had unbelievable deep friendships. I have had good health. I have been honored with the priesthood of Jesus Himself. I have traveled much of the world and been appropriately impressed. I have experienced the thrill of higher education, of teaching on graduate levels, the challenges of modern radio and television broadcasting. I have had the confidences and trust of archbishops, priests, religious brothers, nuns, married people, and single ones, the very young and the very old, the bright and the slow, who have asked me to walk with them through their fears and joys and perplexities. Scientists, police chiefs, Broadway personnel, frightened street people, alcoholics, sexaholics, anorexics, varlets with anorexic sideburns, all have trusted me with their secrets.

In my later life I had the inexpressible privilege to minister to the good Catholic souls of Courage who struggle with the unasked-for disordered tendency of same-sex attraction. Week after week I have been spiritually wide-eyed as I watch the miracle of God's grace transform men of discouragement and despair to men of hope and self-esteem.

Through the mysterious plan of the Lord, I became a local confessor for the fabulous Sisters of Life at the Sacred Heart convent where I had more than privilege or pleasure but deep-seated joy. I saw the beauty of real vocation and the noble lifestyle that confronts the contemporary Christian.

How much joy can the heart hold? Or how does one articulate to the Lord the dimensions of gratitude? How does one put into words one's depth of feeling? Perhaps, there is no way except to stand in awe in His gracious and ineffable presence and be still.

I have been able to recognize my gifts as, as Rush Limbaugh says, on loan from God. I have used them unhesitatingly, with joy and without apology. There is always something missing, to be sure. But that is the meaning of paradise and life with the Lord in eternity. On balance, it has been a really great ride especially for a primitive, dirty-necked kid from the West side. I am filled with gratitude to the Lord and my friends and family. Halleluiah!

Concerning the Soul of Tony Hendra and
Fr. Joe Who Saved It

Aristotle taught that the perfect mathematical figure is the circle since it ends where it began. And someone said that psychoanalysis is the art of missing the obvious. I, as a hoary, arthritic priest/psychologist, had both thoughts upon finishing the brilliantly written and, at times, frighteningly sad book *Father Joe: The Man Who Saved My Soul* (Random House, 2004) by the British writer, Tony Hendra. After wading through the dazzling list of justified and laudatory blurbs, my interest was whetted, not so much to experience Mr. Hendra's formidable writing skills, as to experience his soul or his personhood. I was not disappointed. It was most rewarding, particularly for me, an eight-five-year-old priest who has been practicing psychotherapy for forty years.

With the touching innocence of the black-or-white teenage personality, Tony swung, at different life stages, from one singular certainty to another. At one time he is certain that a torrid, secretive sexual liaison with a married woman is the apex of life. Later, at another time, he is certain that he truly is called to be a celibate contemplative Benedictine monk. At one point he extols the beauty and freedom of chastity, at another he strains for a couple more supererogated orgasms. From a superficial faith life he leaps, almost in an instant, to a halleluiah level: "What had been baffling claptrap all my life suddenly became more than a proposition; it became true and real. I felt a welling overflowing excitement in the perception that "God existed and therefore so did I."[12] Was this the powerful and loving grace of the gracious God or was it a function of a developing young personality or both?

Still, later as an adult, with a kind of cascading "blinders over the eyes" personality, he is certain that his call is to save the world from itself by a slashing, stinging, sometimes even savage life view he called satire. He becomes certain that he must destroy every sacred cow in sight, puncture every pompous balloon and eviscerate every strutting hypocrite on the horizon. Utterly nothing is to be exempt. This glorious mission is to happen through the great medium of laughter, with no holds barred and sensitivity ignored. But it will happen only within a kind of inner-crowd bubble.

It will not be the laughter of the Sam Levenson, Myron Cohen, Fred Allen, Jack Benny genre which gave millions the gift which C.S. Lewis called the belly laugh. It isn't even the laughter of one of my heroes, S.J. Perlman, whose book *Westward Ha!* (with hilarious sketches by Al Herschfeld) became my laughing companion on a long, boring trip on a freighter to Cape Town, to my first Missionary assignment. It isn't the hilarity of Peter Sellers or the comedic genius of Sid Casear or Groucho and his loopy company. Why not? Because it destroys and has a tinge of hate in it. I cannot find it funny. While Fr. Joe taught that "love alone can conquer hate," Tony once said: "I hate love."[13]

It isn't the laughter of my vaudevillian parents, my Jewish father, joking, kidding, teasing or my Irish mother who laughed till it almost hurt. While, sometimes superficial, they were mostly sheer enjoyment. Never were they malicious or hurtful. Is there a substantive difference between laughter at someone and laughter with someone? When eyes don't laugh anymore and humor becomes constricted, forced and ultimately bitter or pitiless, when the humorist gets hard-hearted and uncompassionate, when traces of sadism surface, we have gone too far. Or is it something like the kids writing dirty words on public bathroom walls? Is teenage blasphemy a way of thumbing one's nose at parental figures (even if one is a thirty-year-old teen)? Is it latently about unresolved authority problems thrust deep into one's unconscious life?

Is it psychology which has taught me that I get like what I pay attention to? Or was it my Irish grandmother, educated only to the third grade, who taught me, "Never make fun of what is sacred to someone else"? Pre-articulation and intuition seem to shriek out to me a cautionary signal. It is too complex for a facile explanation; nevertheless, it is comforting to remember my old buddy, Freud, and his "things are rarely only what they seem."

Yet how frightened and sad Tony must have been at one stage: "I was one of the craziest, unhappiest, most vindictive, least trustworthy people I knew. Yikes."[14] But the marvelous monk, Father Joe, with the vast ears and the knobby knees, came to the rescue. He asks Tony (p. 187) about satire and the ideal of straightening out the wayward world: "Does satire often 'bring the bastards down'?" And Tony responds: "Alas, no." It is a puzzlement. How could it happen that a nice, smart Brit kid with a definite (if underdeveloped) attraction to God, with a mystical appreciation of the Eucharist (even through the dirty fingernails of Fr. Bleary) could be so misled? So seduced by false gods? Was it some evil spirit which masked the un-good with the face of laughter?

Where was I, the priest-shrink living in New York, when this good natured, ambiguous Catholic was flailing around, being pursued a la Francis Thompson by the *Hound of Heaven*? "I needed something that I could get nowhere else (Fr. Joe), least of all in New York. A Confessor. A shrink who knew right from wrong: one who would talk while I listened."[15] I was, in God's Providence, doing the spiritual walk with those to whom I was called. This unique Father Joe, no one else, was tailored for this unique Tony Hendra. It was this unique Father Joe who needs a Polish joke explained, who likes a glass of red wine and who is fascinated by blondes, intelligent or otherwise—this is the one who is tapped by the loving Lord as the catalyst for the salvation of a special soul.

It was Father Joe who encouraged Tony to read Meister Eckhart where he found that real laughter is linked to God.

"When God laughs at the soul and the soul laughs back at God, the persons of the Trinity are begotten. When the Father laughs at the Son and the Son laughs back at the Father, that laughter gives pleasure, that pleasure gives joy, that joy gives love and that love is the Holy Spirit."[16]

There is something very arresting in Father Joe's style as a Spiritual Director. He combines "not taking oneself too seriously" with treating the "other with gentleness and respect." His skill in the care of souls is fascinating to me. With my own clinical background, I sense at least a quasi-Rogerian counseling dimension in his priestly ministrations. I didn't hear scolding or lecturing or terrifying or moral frowning. I note his positive language, e.g., "Be unselfish" rather than "Don't be selfish." It strikes me that there is a significant difference here in the tonality. On the contrary, I sensed a deep belief in the goodness of the human being and an enormous trust in the gracious Lord who loves all with an implacable love beyond understanding. There was, it seemed to me, a belief that, in God's good time, Tony would rise to the call of grace. It reminds me of the thinking of my old swimming partner, Dr. Tony Schwarz, who, as the expert in understanding sound, taught the invisible chord theory.

Thus Tony believed that all one must do is find the existent frequency within the soul of the other, play to that chord and the correct music, peace or energy or joy or commitment will emerge. Father Joe, perhaps intuitively or possibly with a special grace of understanding, played this invisible chord on young Tony and on all he met. Actually, the Divine Conductor, I believe, was behind it all.

The young Tony's observational skills were astounding. His delicious description (p. 51) of the Monk Groupies was hilarious and a remarkable bull's eye. These unattractive old Gollum-like types are all over the Catholic world with their superficial, poorly understood theology and their insatiable appetite for daily gossip. Ever more delightful to them would be public scandal within the Church. What a picnic they might have with the thieving monsignor and the ephebophilic priest!

The older Tony arrives at another remarkable and profound truth. Listening. On page 181 he notes: "[L]isten at every level; to the words, the emotions, the intent of the other...be completely open...bring nothing preconceived or prepared to the moment. Listen and then speak only to what you've heard."

"The only way to know God is to listen—listening is the reaching out into that unknown other self...the first exercise in love." And Tony writes this in the Big Apple which he calls "a city of non-listeners." And it does seem that God is always saying: "Be still. Be still."

It is patently clear that Father Joe was a real listener whose two vast ears were not his only mode of hearing. He owned what the shrinks call the third ear. He obviously had deep affection for Tony who becomes, in effect, his son. Their relationship became a deep and loving one whereby whatever deficits Tony's natural father had had were healed. It speaks volumes when Tony describes his anemic familial relationship: "I wasn't used to being held against his tubby body—smelling of the day-old aftershave on his jowls."[17] It is surprising that Tony was not more damaged psychologically.

I have never met Tony, except through this book but I like him. Fr. Joe who knew him exceedingly well, loved him. Clearly before God, he must be lovable. 'Nuff said!

As to Aristotelian metaphor: Tony began with inchoate faith, sincere and true. He winds up in the same faith place, but deeper and truer.

As to psychoanalysis and missing the obvious: Tony's quasi obsession with noses. How did he miss the treasure under his own? In that inchoate faith there were tons of peace and joy, authentic excitement and laughter, meaning and God. The kingdom of the Lord is within. I rejoice that now he knows the real score.

Are There Any Limits to Free Speech or Good Taste?

It is an alleged dogma taught in journalism schools that while all Americans have the basic right to speak out as our insights indicate, we (especially professional journalists) do not have the right to change the facts. This seems a fair and tolerant position which we all cheerfully uphold. The fledging journalist is pummeled to check the facts. He is reminded repeatedly to double check before he commits to publication. Further, the schools cling ferociously to the sacred First Amendment rights of free speech and freedom of the press. It is heartily believed that Americans have almost an absolute right to express themselves at will. But the important and cautious word is almost. It is consensually held, I think, that shouting fire in a crowded theatre when there is no fire is beyond freedom of speech. The shouter knows that his shout is untrue and that others stand to suffer significantly because of his distortion and irresponsibility. He is not constitutionally protected in his shouting.

Likewise, inciting a crowd to a lynching party by twisted or untrue allegations is not constitutionally protected. Nor is a rebellion, fueled by untrue propagandistic material, against a justly installed government legitimate. There are limits to what we call free speech.

Recently, however (May 27, 2006), the usually ethical cable station A&E aired a program which seriously overstepped the bounds of honest journalism, (and I personally believe) of constitutional freedom, and flagrantly offended the spiritual sensitivities of many Christians. The program, meant to focus on some esoteric group called the Illuminati, significantly highlighted a totally one-sided position which was not only anti-

Christian (and heavily anti-Catholic) but, in my mind, worse in that its scholarship was sophomoric and its tonality was bitter. And some of it was blatantly false.

For example, a woman scholar with a straight face asserted that the Catholic claim to Petrine primacy was untrue because Catholicism bases its position on the historical fact that Peter was the first to see the risen Christ. She went on happily stating that John and Mary both saw the risen Jesus before Peter did. Hence, the papal claims are bogus. If she had bothered to check, she, hopefully, would have discovered that the claim is not based on John's Gospel but on Matthew's, 16:19. The most unsophisticated Catholic child in the fourth grade knows this. How come our scholar did not? Or does my psychologist's nose smell something else? Perhaps, she is not interested in the truth or the facts. Is old Sig Freud right again when he suggests that "things are rarely what they seem?" Is the agenda more of hate than light?

The facile assertion that what are claimed to be the bones of Peter might be the bones of an animal is nowhere countered by even a suggestion to the contrary. For fair investigations, the excavations called the scavi under the Basilica of St. Peter, with fifty-five years of serious archeological study, at least should be mentioned. Apart from the pervasive tentative and ambiguous language throughout the whole presentation such as "might," "could be," "some say," "it has been said" (and generally without references), the quick juxtaposition of clips from the Nazi era, subliminally linking the Holy Father with the Fuhrer, clearly suggested a common obsession to control the masses. Both are dictators. Both demand total obedience with no room for individual conscience. The Pope and Hitler, despite the difference of language and garments, are the same. We saw the goose-stepping, seig-heiling Nazis one second, and the crowds in St. Peter's Square applauding the Pope in the next. So, the theme and tone ran. My old Irish

Grandmother who was educated only to the third grade, taught me constantly thusly: "Never make fun of what is sacred to someone else." This is elegance and class. What I saw on A&E was inelegant and crass bad taste. It almost shouted the primitive and low class.

I expected to see the clumsy insertion of the wealth of the Vatican brought out for our consideration. It, of course, popped on the screen—with all the old 19th century anti-Catholic implication. The poor. The sick. The world's poverty. Why isn't it all sold to do good? It is the old Judas Iscariot question. Of course, we never heard, as presented by Dr. William Donahue, of the Catholic League, that the priceless art of the Vatican cannot be translated into dollar signs. It is not sellable. It can't even be used as collateral.

Nor did we hear that the annual operating budget of the Vatican is less than that of Notre Dame University in South Bend. It would be impolite, I suppose, to mention that the wealth of Harvard University is astronomically vaster than the Vatican and Notre Dame combined. Since we are on the track of what is clearly anti-Catholic bias, we could hardly omit the Galileo case. The scholars on A&E blandly asserted that the real reason for the suppression of this scientist was the Church's fear that Catholics would leave the Church and become sun worshippers—a loss of control. It is clearly implied that Catholicism is anti-science. I heard no historical context, nor did I hear of the apology given by Pope John Paul II on behalf of the whole Church. Nor did I hear of Pope John Paul II's encyclical: *Fides et Ratio* on the convergence of religion and science. Nowhere was there any indication of the Academy, the Vatican's worldwide gathering of scientists.

The case of some early Pope mysteriously dying only thirteen days after his election (with dark implications of foul play), the pompous presentation of the worldly Innocent X, the super serious tone in presenting the secular ambitions of warrior Popes, all implied Catholic corruption and deceit. Nowhere did we hear of John Paul II or John XXIII or Gregory the Great or Pius VII. Or any of the many saintly and compassionate Pontiffs of our history. To make such an unbalanced presentation is more than bad taste. It is bigotry.

However, the most outrageous example of this unscholarly presentation was the tentative possibility that perhaps the mummified body of Jesus Christ is kept in a catacomb in Rome which is off limits to researchers. With an incredible violation of Logic 101, it is stated that, because of the limitation, perhaps there is something to this possibility. I recall the old saw that, since the burned body could not be absolutely verified to be that of the Fuehrer, perhaps Adolph Hitler escaped the bunker to live out his days in Argentina with Eva Braun. He dyed his mustache, grew it longer and wore dark glasses. Some people believed it, fearing that he might return. Others, unconsciously, wanted it to be true. Most people said: "Baloney. It is an obvious fantasy." The interest in the touted novel, *The Da Vinci Code* (Dan Brown, Anchor 2009), is huge even though it is obvious fantasy. Some people might want it to be true. But for a journalist to assert its authenticity knowing that it is sheer imagination is to be dishonest.[18]

The possibility that anyone can be mistaken is taken for granted. However, professionals are supposed to be adult enough to acknowledge an error, to accept the new proven information and make the correction. But knowingly to mislead the gullible is not only dishonest but evil. The misleading is not necessarily frontal but, more insidiously, oblique. For example, the program noted, with a critical tone, that when researchers are given access to priceless documents in the Vatican archives, they are carefully watched by a cleric. The show made an obvious and false implication. They don't want you to know the real truth. What does one expect when viewing priceless documents? Beer and bagels? The *Magna Carta* would not be available for any college undergraduate at his simple request without serious supervision.

If this A&E presentation were just shoddy research, it could be easily overlooked as the awkward attempt of some historical or theological bumpkin to make his mark in modern television. This presentation has all the penumbras and emanations of bigotry. The errors and distortions might be understandable in 1858 in the days of Know Nothingism. Today, there are too many opportunities to check assertions before any kind of serious publication. Otherwise, the presenters of this program might be suffering from an unresolved juvenile repression surfacing today as uncovering the real truth of Christianity. It sounds a lot like embedded teenage rebellion. Perhaps, they had better look me up professionally for psychotherapy. My number is in the New York telephone directory. My fees are light and my burden is Truth.

Should We Cohabitate Before Marriage?

Often when I have questioned the prudence of young people considering cohabitation before marriage, I am met with the quizzical look and the now remark: "C'mon, Father, get real." I am told that living together before marriage is a good way for couples "to find out whether they really get along." I am reminded of the high cost of living and how two can live more cheaply than one and that everyone is doing it. Marriage is just a piece of paper anyway. What's the difference? Besides, it's good preparation for marriage. And all the facile, mindless bromides and rationalizations that pass as street smarts. This is popular thinking as evidenced, for example, in a national survey of high-school seniors which found nearly sixty percent approving this trend. In fact, a new report shows that half of all first marriages are now preceded by cohabitation.

The Catholic Church, however, has traditionally insisted that marriage is a holiness producing institution, a sacrament, and that the sexual component is truly holy but strictly reserved for a man and a woman in this specific state of marriage. Cohabitation is, in this view, inappropriate (or more bluntly, sinful, as is any use of sex outside of marriage). Obviously, such a stance in this era is counter-cultural, almost radical. Of course, some young Catholic couples disobey their Church and do cohabit before marriage and sometimes even substitute such a relationship for marriage. They join the four million unmarried couples now living together (compared with less than half a million forty years ago.) Clearly, they act counter to Catholic teaching.

But it is heartening to read of the monumental study out of Rutgers University (Feb. 2006) which challenges the popular thinking by publishing the opposite viewpoint. This study runs utterly opposite to the cheerful illusion that it doesn't really matter whether couples cohabit before marriage. I have heard some uninformed Catholic priests make such observations (perhaps I should say non-confrontational or peace-at-any-price priests). But this professional challenge is based on sociological and psychological grounds, not on religious ones. Somehow, the voices of the secular are heard long before the clarity of God's will.

It is entitled: "Should we live together before marriage? What young adults need to know about cohabitation before marriage."[19] As part of the New Jersey schools' National Marriage Project, researchers David Popenoe and Barbara Dafoe Whitehead conclude that "cohabitation does not reduce the likelihood of eventual divorce; in fact, it may lead to a higher divorce rate."

Their major findings include the following:

1. Living together before marriage increases the risk of breaking up after marriage.

2. Unmarried couples have lower levels of happiness and well-being than married couples.

3. Living together outside of marriage increases the risk of domestic violence and the risk of physical and sexual abuse for children.

While these findings are factual, the reasons for their reality are not clear. What underlies the findings? Why is this so? The authors state: "Although cohabiting relationships are like marriages—they typically differ in the levels of commitment and autonomy involved." The results obviously did surprise many people but the report stated: "Perhaps the most obvious explanation for the striking statistical association between cohabitation and divorce is that the people willing to cohabit are more unconventional than others and less committed to the institution of marriage." Professionally, I can recall from my many marital counseling cases how often the roles of commitment and autonomy formed the fundamental core of interpersonal discord. But how much more so must it be with cohabitating couples who have anemic commitment and infantile notions of autonomy?

I submit the glaring case of two Catholics living together for a year with huge interpersonal problems. She, with a fancy Catholic college background and desperately wanting marriage, he, an inactive lawyer with a comfortable trust fund on which to live, with an obsession for roller skating, expensive restaurants and no interest in marrying. They had low commitment and high self-centered autonomy. When they consulted me for a mediation, he blatantly stated to her: "I have no responsibility to you. I owe you nothing." This after a full year of living together with required sexual intimacy. With an infantile *idée fixe*, he insisted that sex was better without marriage. Marriage, with all its added responsibilities, would only spoil the pleasure. He asks: "Why rock the boat?" Does it take a Henry Kissinger I.Q. level to predict the future of this relationship?

The shrill ever present modern battle cry "I have a right to happiness" rings hollow here. Their happiness level was abysmal even as their grim sexual life was rapidly becoming jaded.

Apparently, the pattern of low commitment and high autonomy is hard to unlearn. Popenoe and Whitehead, along with other researchers found that the cohabitation attitude, which is pervasively operational in these couplings, changes people's view of marriage itself. The study suggests that cohabitation moves people either to make marriage less likely or if marriage takes place to make it less successful.

That specter lurking in the background of cohabitating life is always whispering sotto voce the anytime-breakup possibility. With no strings attached either partner can pack up and steal away into the sunset seeking the elusive "Mr./Ms. Right." Should this occur, the battering and bruising of the psyche (especially of a woman) can be incalculable. Obviously, there are no real assurances in cohabitation where commitment is so essentially tenuous. This is particularly problematic in the case of the serial cohabitor. The authors have concluded "the experience of dissolving one cohabitation for another generates a greater willingness to dissolve later relationships." Hence, less real commitment and greater risk for a future marriage.

It is stated that the study may hold the answer to the question why pre-marital cohabitation should affect the stability of a later marriage. Despite its intrinsic narcissism, the "I owe you nothing" message is the warp and woof of cohabitation. When the young guy says to me, "Get real, Father," how can I help him see the reality of the dangers of cohabitation? I'm sure no one is totally immune from his environment so how could this underlying sense of instability not influence a cohabitating relationship?

The elephant in the living room of this problem is assiduously avoided by those who beat the politically correct drum. The elephant is the low level of happiness of the cohabitors. This study courageously faces what happens within the relationship itself. Get this surprising finding: "Cohabiting couples report lower levels of happiness, lower levels of sexual exclusivity and sexual satisfaction, and poorer relationships with their parents." It is also noted that within two years, about half of all cohabiting relationships are terminated. It is either complete breakup or marriage. And after five years, only about ten percent of couples are still cohabiting.[20]

It is noted that the annual rates of depression among cohabiting couples are more than three times that of married couples. Further, women in these relationships are more likely than married women to suffer physical and sexual abuse. These statistics indicate that aggression is at least twice as high among cohabitors as it is among married people.

A British study (quoted by the authors) found that "compared to children living with married biological parents, children living with cohabiting but unmarried biological parents are twenty times more likely to be subject to child abuse, and those living with a mother and a cohabiting boyfriend who is not the father face an increased risk of thirty-three times. In contrast, the rate of abuse is fourteen times higher if the child lives with a biological mother who lives alone."

Those who are concerned about the welfare of children might well ponder the concluding statement: "[T]he evidence suggests that the most unsafe of all family environments of children is that in which the mother is living with someone other than the child's biological father. This is the environment for the majority of children in cohabiting couple households."

Where is the outrage from the media? Where are the flamboyant champions of children's rights? Why has this information not been publicized? I thought that the public has a right to know the truth. Is there some kind of slanted, selective reporting at work here? I recall the outcry when the Catholic Church opposed the use of condoms in Africa as the means to contain AIDS. While a detour from the focus of this paper, the example illustrates my bewilderment. The Church was assailed by the usual invectives: backward, anti-progressive, un-real, non-compassionate. All the usual pejorative adjectives. But why, in this case, wasn't I told the whole truth? For example, that South Africa has reached a twenty-two percent infection level of the entire population in spite of a massive inundation of condoms? Or that Botswana where condom sales rose from one million to three million now has a rise in HIV-infection cases from twenty-seven percent to forty-five percent among pregnant women? Or that Uganda with a forty-three percent Catholic population has four percent HIV-infected adults following not condom use but abstinence? Uganda uses the national motto: "Change your behavior, change your behavior." Why am I not told the truth? Was the repression of the facts based on personal bias?

This media selectivity covers up the truth about cohabitation. The truth is: "If you want to be married for a lifetime, then you should know that cohabitating promotes the opposite outcome." And as the Rutgers report says: "Despite its widespread acceptance by the young, the remarkable growth of unmarried cohabitation in recent years does not appear to be in children's or society's best interests. The evidence suggests it has weakened marriage and the intact two-parent family and thereby damaged our social wellbeing, especially that of women and children."

If current society were to have no real interest in maintaining a fairly healthy level of the marriage state, we would not only have gone collectively insane but we would also be committing massive social suicide. It would mean the end of the American experiment as we have known it. The perspicacious among us are fueling the movement to educate American youth not only about the dangers of cohabitation but also about the drive for same-sex marriage. Both corruptions are serious enemies of marriage. The country should know this. The hypothesis of the study follows: "[S]ociety wide, the growth of cohabitation will tend to further weaken marriage as an institution...particularly if one or both parties had cohabitated with someone else or brought children into the relationship."

Can we get the word out? Can we stop institutionalizing cohabitation and get back to revitalizing marriage? How do we publicize the findings of sociology and psychology as they try to catch up with the wisdom of God? After all, it was the Lord Jesus who made marriage a Sacrament. I don't recall Him ever attending parties for fornicators or sodomites! When the Lord God gave the Ten Commandments to Moses, He did not stipulate a time limit or statute of limitation after which cohabitation and same-sex unions would become holy. C'mon, USA, get really real!

Was There Really a Priest Pedophile Problem?

I knew a battled hardened old Paulist debater, Fr. James M. Gillis, who used to thunder at priests-in-the-making that we must insist on definition before we discuss any matter of serious import. A basic finding in debate research, he taught, is that the victory belongs to him who frames the debate.

In striving for precise definition and intelligent debate, it is essential to know the difference between the connotative and the denotative meanings of words. The connotations of a word can range all over the verbal landscape and can apply to all kinds of marginal meanings, including that which the listener might wish to inject into a concept. It can be a kind of Rorschach journey, akin to looking at floating clouds and giving a personal meaning or perception to each. On the other hand, the denotative meaning of a word is specific and univocal. There is practically and usually no other meaning to it. A debater might unethically use a word in a connotative sense and hope that his opponent doesn't pick up his somewhat sloppy intellectual behavior. This occurs more than we like to admit. Unless one is used to demanding definition, it is highly possible that exchanges move off into what has been called airy persiflage. There is no common ground achieved but only hardening of respective positions despite fancy talk and impassioned articulation. All of us, certainly including this writer, must be honest in the use of our terms if we are to be faithful to the spirit of the Lord and be helpful to others.

One fascinating example of the misuse of language, deliberate or otherwise, surfaced many times in the priest scandal reporting. This was the imprecise use of the word pedophile which has a denotative and specific scientific meaning. The word itself, taken from Greek roots, in the world of psychology, refers to the sexual molestation of and attraction to pre-pubertal persons—i.e., before puberty, roughly and denotatively prior to the age of twelve. The philia or love is toward children who are younger than the stage of puberty. This is vastly and substantively different from being sexually attracted to adolescent or teenage persons.

Hence, when the media or special interest groups refer to the priest pedophile scandal, they are inaccurate or, more precisely, incorrect. The overwhelming majority of these cases has involved persons in the teen years, anywhere from fourteen to nineteen. The professional categorization for teen age sexual molestation is called Ephebophilia, again from Greek roots, specifically and denotatively, meaning sexual attraction to older adolescents.

This distinction is well known and easily verifiable. So, the blurring of the word-usage is somewhat puzzling. In a recent public lecture, I gave on the roots of same-sex attraction[21] (homosexuality), I attempted to clarify the distinction (using perhaps a barbed wire approach) that there wasn't a pedophile scandal at all but a homosexual one. A person who apparently identifies himself as gay was deeply upset by my distinction and wished to peg the word pedophile on the unfaithful priests. In the dialogue with him, it became clear that since both sick heterosexuals and sick homosexuals are probably equally guilty of molesting little children, the gay world preferred to label the priest thing as pedophilia thereby shifting the focus away from homosexuality. The hype stance was: "Don't blame us (gays)—blame the Church."

Actually, the media (and many gay-friendly lawyers) often employ a very elastic and connotative use of the word pedophilia to include anyone under the age of twenty-one. However, when the studies (particularly the John Jay report) came out clearly indicating that anywhere between 80 percent and 90 percent of the cases since 1950 have involved homosexual priests, there was a wild scurrying about to fog up the findings. We were told that these were not really homosexual priests but only priests seeking some kind of sexual discharge and the young men were the nearest sexual experience they could have without women. Whatever the internal tensions of these priests were, the descriptive word generally applied to an adult male having sex with a teen aged male is homosexual. In the mood of the old story, perhaps the king does have a beautiful suit on but he looks stark naked, not only to kids but to most people whose eyes are open.

Occasionally, some courageous and independent-minded journalists break out of the conformist mold and dare to confront the facts. One such was Joe Fitzgerald of the *Boston Herald* on March 11, 2002 when he blatantly entitled his column "Homosexuality is True Plague of Priesthood" which, predictably, raised the proverbial hackles of the gay Catholic community. He wrote "[M]ilitant homosexuals and their timorous allies in the politically correct movement are hell-bent on perpetuating the disingenuous notion that the crisis engulfing the Catholic Church has its roots in pedophilia. It does not. It has its roots in homosexuality, and to call it anything else is to insult the intelligence of anyone who's paying attention, especially anyone with access to a dictionary."

Even granting a touch of paranoia on my part, I have noticed the media tendency to imply not only that this is an on-going problem with Catholic priests but that it is massive in nature. The accurate (honest and fair?) appraisal is that the tragedy of these homosexual priests reached its apex in the 1970-1985 period, that it is, in a real sense, unhappy ancient history and that the situation has improved enormously. Why don't we hear such statements in the media? Is there an agenda signaled by the word blurring, e.g., pedophilia and the little remarks about priest pedophiles periodically sneaked into some piece of Catholic news?

Recently, Cardinal Egan, the Archbishop of New York made the following public statement:[22]

"We must never lose sight of the fact the Archdiocese of New York has an extraordinary presbyterate and that our record is very likely the best in the nation. When compiling the list of allegations for the national audit, the Archdiocese amounted to less than 1 percent of the thousands of priests who have served and continue to serve the Archdiocese for the past fifty plus years. The New York City Public Schools, on the other hand, had more allegations of sexual abuse of minors by teachers in the first semester of this academic year alone than the Archdiocese has had in more than fifty years."

Dr. William Donahue, President of the Catholic Defense League and a professional sociologist, observes that in the year 2005, there were twenty-one allegations that involved minors as victims but only five were found credible, two were still under investigation and in two other instances, there was insufficient information. Ultimately, there were at most nine priest cases for the year. He notes that we had approximately 42,000 priests in 2005 which means that 0.02% had a credible accusation made against him. One unfaithful priest is too many for me, but the facile implication of widespread abuse (by misuse of words and mindless statements) is dishonest and unjust. Why wasn't it reported that in 2005, 99.98% of the priests in the United States had no credible accusation made against them? It was nowhere reported. Incidentally, Dr. Donahue sharply reminds us that the term ephebophile is never used to refer to heterosexual acts, only homosexual ones.[23] The term is probably ideologically coined and rarely used. But it is precise in its meaning. The overwhelming percentage of the heinous acts by those erring priests was with adolescent males. There have been feeble insinuations that priests will now molest altar girls but the interesting fact is that after twelve years of females serving at the altar, there are no such problems. As Donahue points out "[I]t is still the males that the molesters want."

Dr. Donahue makes the bold assertion: "I am willing to bet that there is no institution, demographic group or profession in the United States today that has less of a problem with sexual abuse of minors than the Catholic Church." So, from where come the vicious attacks? And why?

Obviously, there is some open, outright prejudice against the Catholic Church as Dr. Philip Jenkins of Penn State so brilliantly proved in his *The New Anti-Catholicism: The Last Acceptable Prejudice*.[24] This type of enemy is tolerable. The more serious and difficult to understand is the enemy within. In World War II, we were all familiar with the term of disgrace: "Quisling" which meant the enemy within our own ranks, pretending to be loyal to our cause but secretly working to destroy us, with full understanding or not.

It looks like we have the deepest problem with our own troops. One of the clear implications of the recent Vatican document establishing criteria for evaluating SSA seminary candidates, was the likely tendency of such candidates to have a false tolerance (such as that described by Rev. David Kennedy of Florida as the "last virtue of a degenerate society") or even encouragement of intrinsically sinful behavior. The Catholic Church teaches that homosexual behavior[25] is intrinsically immoral and can, in no circumstances, ever be approved.

Yet, resistance from within remains a factor. How can one explain priest-confessors (in the sacrament of Penance itself) advising SSA penitents that they should not be hasty in breaking up same-sex relationships (read sexual)? Or advising that God understands their sinning? How come a pastor in a gay neighborhood will become visibly indignant when he is challenged by a Courage member on the pastor's refusal to discuss chastity from the pulpit? How come that pastor suggests to his challenger that he "go somewhere else for Mass"? How come another pastor will sugarcoat the Catholic teaching because the gays in his parish give generously whenever he needs money? How come another pastor, with reputed ambiguous gender identity, will call Fr. John Harvey, loyal son of the Church and real founder of Courage, "a bastard" when Harvey will reveal, with permission, frightening information given by Courage members? How come a Catholic bishop announces publicly that he will no longer discuss the Church's position on homosexual behavior lest it bother gay sensitivity?

Is this masking? Or lying? Is it that gender confusion/arrested development are in the clergy itself? Asking challenging and even uncomfortable questions will not surface all the causation of the problem. Nor will it reveal forms of resolution. It will, however, reveal the name of the real problem.

This is a serious situation. It is more than mere semantics or arguing about verbal nuances. The meanings under the words carry huge social and spiritual import. So, the question in the title, "Was there really a priest pedophile problem?" is rhetorical. If the reader followed the reasoning presented above, it is obvious. Homosexual, yes. Pedophile, no. No wonder Church leaders are concerned about the sexual identity of priest personnel. If I were Pope, God forbid, I would be extremely concerned. Wouldn't you?

The Mysterious and Inexplicable "Pull" of Jewishness

Although only half of my being is Jewish since I had a Russian-Jewish father and an Irish mother, I have felt throughout my life a pull or draw (which I can't explain) to the warmth, energy, laughter and loyalty to whatever we mean by Jewish. This tendency is all the more amazing to me since I am a Catholic priest, totally devoted to my faith, delighted with the joys of Catholic spirituality and convinced that Catholicism is the fullness of religion as revealed by God, bar none.

Yet, I have a mezuzah on the door post to my office which I touch reverently as I begin my day of counseling God's suffering children. I have two yarmulkes which I use at appropriate times. I love Jewish humor and I love to hang out with Jewish friends. I bristle and suffer when someone makes an anti-Semitic remark, particularly when the bigot has no idea of my Jewish side since, as they tell me, "You look so Irish."

A snide remark about the Jews is an attack not only on the Jews but particularly on my father and on me! Never mind that such bigotry is insulting to my Jewish Lord, Jesus, and His holy Jewish Mother and all my Biblical heroes, the big fisherman, sweaty Peter and the bald-headed, bandy-legged enthusiastic Paul and John and Mary Magdalene as well as later pals, like Edith Stein, among so many others. It is also insulting to my Catholicism which declares such behavior to be overtly sinful. Certainly, my own instant rising to the challenge is not only my conscious Catholicism but also, I suppose, the unconscious awareness that had I been in Dachau in 1938, I, too, could have ended up in the oven. Irish looking or not. Devout Catholic or not. I definitely have Jewish blood. I must wear the Star of David on my sleeve and declare myself as Juden.

As a kid, during the devastating economic depression, my father, mother, sister and I worked Jewish hotels in the Jewish alps (the Catskills) as the social staff. We could get no other form of income. The Jews provided one. We sang, danced, did skits, juggled, and ran bingo games for the old Jewish gals. We ate kosher food in which case I would scandalize the good simple Jewish waiter (Emil, with the heavy Central European accent) when I insisted on having a glass of milk with meat. I have never forgotten the warmth and cordiality and these Jewish good times from my adolescent years.

Yet the attraction can hardly be environmental when I recall that I was forbidden to meet my Jewish grandparents because I was a clearly defined Christian (even an altar boy).[26] I had little Jewish contact apart from the summer jobs. My name had been changed from Rosenbloom (my birth name) to Lloyd. I was brought up in a totally Christian, non-Jewish world. I was identified de facto as Gentile, not Jewish. How come this almost mystical feeling in me?

I even recall one of my Christian relatives, a good, simple, uneducated man, utterly without thinking, would shout "Ya Jew Bastard" at anyone who would cut him off. The offending motorist could be black, yellow or brown, Catholic, atheist or animist. Somehow he had co-mingled an unarticulated anti-Semitism with low tolerance for conflict into this automatic epithet. Of course, he had easy access to similar putdowns for blacks, Poles, Italians and Puerto Ricans. If he had had any other ethnic makeup than his own, I am sure he would easily have been able to classify the Irish as donkeys and micks.

I, as a psychologist, am very much aware of identity formulation. Even my good friend and colleague, Dr. Arnie Zucker, who is very Jewish[27] and a psychiatrist, frequently sings into the ears of his twin grandchildren to solidify their Jewish identity. Believing that behavioral data, even at this early age, will be recorded deep in their young psyches, he sings them little ditties like: "Aren't you glad that you are a little Jewish boy? Aren't you glad you were not born a goy?" While some observers believe that the term "goy" is itself an ethnic putdown, nevertheless the process of identity is taking place.

I have probed my own identity formation and asked why do I feel so protective of things Jewish? Whence this kind of pride I feel in Jewish history? I personally revel in the knowledge that such a small percentage of the human race has made such incredible contributions to the world. While I cannot equate everything which is Jewish with the state of Israel, I am amazed how such a tiny country, outnumbered and besieged by hostile neighbors, has been able to give to the world so much of what makes life joyous and livable. I see the startling non-correlation between a small world Jewish population and their disproportionate representation in various fields. Out of a relatively tiny ethnic population comes a large percentage of Jews in professional fields like medicine, law, the arts, education, and certainly business.

How often I have heard the off-hand remark: "Go get yourself a good Jewish lawyer" meaning, I suppose that this would ensure a more pleasing outcome than if one hired a non-Jewish attorney. The compassionate human concern of the Jewish physician is legendary. The dominance of Jewish comedians has been obvious especially to me with my show biz background. How often have I enjoyed belly laughs with Sid Caesar, Mel Brooks, Alan King, Henny Youngman, Uncle Miltie Berle, Don Rickles, Jackie Mason and on and on and on. Even within the world of sports, I enjoyed in my early youth the antics of Jewish boxers like Maxie Baer, Benny Leonard, and Slapsie Maxie Rosenbloom. I remember the great Hank Greenberg with the Detroit Tigers and the All-American running back, Marshall Goldberg, at the University of Pittsburgh. In effect, I am very aware that positive Jewish influence is very widespread, certainly in the history of the United States.

I find myself rooting for Israel and praying for her safety and success. I am nauseated by remarks such as the one made by the president of a European country that Israel is an insignificant "sh—y little country." My reactions are as if I were fully Jewish and an Israeli. Why is this?

Some years ago when I was hosting a television interview show for WNBC in New York, my guest was Fr. Dr. John Oesterricher, the Founder and Director of the Institute for Judeo-Christian Studies at Seton Hall University. My concern and interest was to explore the identity of the Jew. He, a convert to Catholicism with a Germanic background, in response to my question "What is a Jew?" spoke of "people." He dismissed notions of race, nationality, religion and the like. We are a people, he said. He was a devoted and convinced Catholic priest but he was a Jew and always would be. To him the notion of people hood transcends other specifics. He did not believe that Judaism and Jewish-ness are coterminous. Nor do I.

Yet is there some kind of spiritual gene? Is there something in the spirit of people which is passed on to descendants? I, with wide eyed amazement, read Thomas Cahill's carefully written *The Gifts of the Jews* (Anchor Books 1999). Clearly, God has chosen Jews to be His own people. I, as a Catholic, believe I incorporate the basic and, perhaps, inchoate will of God as found in Biblical history. I understand and admire the deep loyalty to family and community which Jews have for their own people. Franz Werfel, Jewish author and admirer of Catholicism described why he could not become a Catholic as much as he was so inclined. To leave his people in their hour of need and join the other side would be, in a sense, a betrayal. The pull for the people of God is enormously strong. I know it. I feel it. I am the anomaly. I am fiercely Catholic and consciously Jewish. And I like it even if I can't really explain it.

Who Are These Christian Brothers?

I was a fourteen-year-old graduate of the Paulist Grammar School where I was protected and taught by the loving and maternal Holy Cross Sisters. Soon, I was to be thrown into the care of some mysterious, tall, black robed men known as the Irish Christian Brothers.[28] It was rumored that each one of them had a brown strap hidden in his robes which he would whip out at the slightest provocation. Teenaged boys allegedly trembled in fear at the very sight of this tool of control. Horror stories of beatings and strange goings on swept our neighborhood. I was in a near panic.

My good Jewish father had wanted me to go to nearby Commerce High school where I would learn business basics for making it in this tough world. Besides, it was free. No tuition. No fees. All the freebies one would need. And, on the other hand, the brothers at this fancy sounding school, Power Memorial Academy, would charge ten dollars a month. And they taught useless stuff like English Literature, French, Latin and Religion!

However, my simple Irish Catholic mother, though usually acquiescing to my father's wishes, stamped and stomped her way to my enrolling at a Catholic High school. With marvelous trust in the Almighty, she knew that although we had no money, somehow the Lord would figure out a way of digging up that enormous sum each month. And, of course, the Lord came through in the person of a gentle Paulist Father, Fr. Paul Ward, who paid my tuition for the four years, enabling me to have one of the most satisfying, productive educational experiences of my life.

The school was located in Harlem, on 124th street right off Lenox Avenue. Power Memorial Academy was actually three or four crummy looking, old brownstone houses. And into them were crammed several hundred boys, a cramped lunchroom in the basement, a tiny chapel on the second floor, classrooms where walls had been broken down to accommodate the young scholars, a back yard passing as recreation space adorned with primitive basketball hoops and, of course, quarters for the brothers.[29] It was not Phillips Exeter or Fordham Prep but we all loved it.

These men had unbelievable dedication to the kids. They were superb educators. They were strong masculine role models and exemplars of faith. They did demand excellence in scholarship which resulted in an impressive record of college scholarships and generally a sense of how to study for the students. The stories of beatings were largely mythical, the kind of exaggeration one might hear sitting before the fireplace on a winter's night. If the strap was used at all, it was largely symbolic, amounting to no more than a slight sting on the hand. It never destroyed the psyche as is claimed by the contemporary bleeding hearts of public schools. On the contrary, most of the boys who got so disciplined knew they deserved it and understood its meaning. It was not only justice but love. It helped us mature and become truly masculine. One need only check the reactions of power alumni over the years to realize how strong was the bond between the brothers and students.

I needed ten cents each day for the subway in addition to my homemade sandwich which I always found in my satchel through the courtesy of my mother (or grandmother when Mom was away on a job). Here I learned the practical meaning of "God will provide" or, as the brothers taught me, *Deus Providebit*. I never worried about the daily dime or the sandwich. I knew they would be there. It left me free to enjoy the thrill of learning about Caesar and Vercingetorix, the dynamics of the quadratic equation, the fluid sound of *"Bon jour, mes enfants,"*[30] the fun of Shakespeare and the endless excitement of the opened mind. It also pervasively taught me, almost like osmosis, what it means to be a Catholic.

Where in God's providence did these guys come from? How did they wind up in the inner city teaching dirty necks like me the basics of reading, writing and computing? What made them tick?

It started in County Waterford, Ireland with a layman named Edmund Rice (1762-1844), a prosperous businessman whose wife had died leaving him with a seriously ill daughter. It was a time when his land had been oppressed by foreign powers leaving the Irish impoverished and generally uneducated. This man who had a lively devotion to the Mother of God, the Blessed Mother, decided to spend some time teaching the many urchins floundering aimlessly around Waterford, giving them some skills in making a living. He did teach them basic computation and reading but it was always against the background of the Catholic Faith. Edmund who has been declared Blessed by the Catholic Church believed in the eternal destiny of all, while at the same time being apparently a hardheaded merchant who knew how to turn pig's ear into a silk purse. He was a believer who like all saints will have empty pockets and impossible dreams but will dare to challenge the common sense of the world.

His charisma, wonderful to most, insane to others, drew scores of goodhearted men who eventually developed into that congregation then called Irish Christian Brothers and now the Congregation of Christian Brothers. No longer just Irish[31] but Indian, African, Australian, American, Hispanic and even English names dot the international roster of the congregation.

But it is always the spirit and vision of Rice which dominates the monks. Although they number noted scholars in their ranks, they all commit to caring for the young. Recently, I had dinner with an old friend who, as a teenager, was totally disoriented relative to his future. By some strange twist of God's plan, Ray entered Power Memorial and indeed was truly saved. A young Br. "Boney" Power took him over, directed him personally and educationally, to a career in the Board of Education of New York City where he became an able and successful leader. Now in retirement he openly (and often) states that his life was saved by Br. Power. Once a confused agnostic, he is today a practicing and proud Catholic. This is the plan of Edmund Rice and one which has been realized thousands of times around the world since those difficult early days in Waterford.

In my years in South Africa, my initial impression of these monks was reenforced and highlighted endless times. They ran the prototypic high level secondary school in Kimberly, the number one school in the country. The Headmaster, Br. McManus was called "Mr. Education" nationwide. He was consulted by government ministers as the ultimate source of what to do in this field. I gave an annual retreat to them at Kimberly, went on vacation with them, played tennis with them and shared their lives as much as a non-monk could. But it was always the same. Dedication. Faith. Commitment to the young. Continual Study. True fraternity. Edmund Rice was written all over them.

I met them in Fiji where they ran a top-level school in the inner city for the indigenous children. They greeted me with warmth and hospitality, even introducing me to the bitter local brew as the natives clapped their hands in delight. I met them in Hawaii where they run a top school for American kids of that area. I was welcomed as their brother and shared their food and shelter. Edmund Rice, who probably never left Ireland physically, was spiritually right there smiling and encouraging them. I met them in Sydney, Australia, where they invited me to share my thoughts at their National Education Convention. Edmund. Edmund. Edmund. He was always there also, urging, challenging, even demanding his spiritual sons to carry on the message of Jesus.

In my own years at the Academy, I was obviously drawn to become Brother Lloyd, so attractive and symbiotic to me was their life It was all I ever yearned for—with one monumental exception. I had a huge and undeniable need to celebrate the Holy Sacrifice of the Mass. Why couldn't I be a brother and priest at the same time?[32] I understand very well that the vocation to be a brother is a special and separate call. When Br. John Mark Egan, the superb Christian psychologist, was asked why he didn't become a priest and go all the way, he correctly and profoundly replied: "Then I couldn't be a Brother." In the mysterious and beautiful makeup of the Mystical Body of Jesus, there are different and equal calls as the Blessed Apostle Paul tells us.

Perhaps, one of the three greatest human beings of my life was Br. A.A. Loftus (called Austie by the insiders). No one so deeply influenced me on multiple levels. He is the one who invited me to "come along with us," i.e., join the monks. Like so many others, I wanted to be like him. He was an incredible scholar who taught me Virgil's *Aeneas*, solid geometry[33], trig, American History, Catholic theology, Cicero's orations on Cataline, the Odes and Epodes of Horace. All on superior levels of teaching. He was a topflight athletic coach winning in successive years the City championships in both basketball and baseball. He was extremely devout in his faith, deeply Catholic, loyal to the Magisterium. Yet, as with many intellectuals, he relaxed with detective stories and Yankee ball games in the stadium.

If he was displeased with us, we were exceedingly uncomfortable. His approval was essential. When as an insufferable big shot senior of seventeen, I was goofing off (slacking in my studies), he ordered me to school on a Saturday intending to whack me over the bottom. As I bent over the desk, with my knees quivering, his basic sensitivity took over and he relented with a verbal reprimand. I had been on the verge of leaving school in mid-year, possibly for a dead-end and mediocre life. Austie set me straight for what I consider my own great ride.

Austie, the Ph.D. par excellence, became the professor of philosophy at Iona College, later president of the College, later Provincial of the Brothers of North America and finally, the top dog, the Superior General of the worldwide Congregation. After his retirement, I met him at Power; in fact in the Brothers Chapel where he sat mystically gazing at his Eucharistic Lord in the tabernacle. I had been deeply impressed as a teenager at his bouncing into the little Chapel at Power before class, oodles of books under his arm, with a quick genuflection asking the Master's guidance on his day. I asked him if he was planning to return to Iona to teach philosophy. He laughingly replied that he was going to a high school because "that is where all the fun is." It was in a high school chapel that he was stricken and quickly was taken to his Lord and Master.

I have been invited several times to preach the annual retreat to the monks at Power, Iona and elsewhere. It has been a strange feeling for me to see the wise, holy, wonderful monks sitting before me listening with incredible humility to my words on the spiritual life. There was Br. Tom Perry at ninety with his hand cupped to his ear least he miss any of my spiritual gems(?). It was he who taught me French, English composition and basic theology! There was the genial, scholarly Br. Blondie Vaughan who taught me about the angles and triangles of plane geometry. There were provincials and scholars and skilled professors listening with some pride to one of their boys.

For ten years in my own retirement, I was privileged to say Mass for these brothers as they became old and infirm. In a beautiful facility run by the brothers themselves, the grand old men who gave so much of their love, talent and faith for others wait patiently for their call to the Lord. Even with age and illness burdening them, they almost automatically radiate Edmund's spirit. They are for others. They always welcomed me, their brother who was a priest as one of their own, making me feel at home with them. Sometimes, they made me laugh as did the Alzheimeric brother who ran up to me one morning to announce that he was getting married the next day. I kiddingly asked if his bride was good looking, and he replied with a satisfied and beaming "absolutely." Others I comforted and encouraged as they worried about their very few inadequacies prior to meeting God. I was so grateful to minister to my dear friend, Br. Alexander Thomas, as he lay dying in the Hawthorne hospice. He with whom I had so much fun competing in bridge games and who in his own way taught me so many of the delights that God provides—the cigar, the goblet with Grand Marnier, and the French jokes.

So many wonderful memories I have of these good men, these sons of Edmund, these champions of and believers in young people. Who are these Christian Brothers? How much time does one have to listen? "*Arma virumque cano*," I sing of religious men and their battle against ignorance, bigotry, coldness and that which is not of God.

It has been my pleasure and privilege along with literally thousands of others to say: "I know them and they know me." May God be praised.

Eating in Restaurants and Finding God!
Or, Is Calling Myself a Spiritual Materialist Oxymoronic?

Since I was a mere stripling of fifteen or so, I have been delighted with Hilaire Belloc's[34] little ditty: "Wherever the Catholic sun doth shine/ there's dancing and laughter and good red wine/ at least I have always found it so/ *Benedicamus Domino*. My delight stems, I think, from my deep-seated Catholic sense of the essential goodness of the material and its intended synthesis with the spiritual. I believe that both matter and spirit are basically good. My scriptural background does clearly indicate that God looked upon what He had done and said, "It is very good." (Gen.1:31). This certainly includes "matter," that which we call the material.

Catholics believe that evil often surfaces, not from the material itself, but from the misuse and misdirection of things thus differing from the plan of the Creator. The dour, grim, unsmiling deviation which one sometimes finds in neurotic Catholics (and certainly in those other religions which doggedly chase witches, drunks and gamblers who smoke) is hardly within our real tradition. It is not alcohol, betting, sex or food, per se, which are intrinsically evil. It is the way we use them which causes departure from the Lord. Drunkenness, gluttony, avarice, lust, covetousness are all offenses before God, caused not by things but by the perverse will of the human being. However and obviously, there is a profound tendency in all of us to misuse the gifts of the earth.

In theological circles this tendency is called original sin. An adult spiritual life, seeking healthy balance, contains and controls such a tendency. The Blessed Apostle Paul recommends a little wine for the sake of the stomach. We teach that sexual love between a husband and wife is holy and righteously to be enjoyed. This is incarnational theology or the role of the physical in the great plan of God. Limited betting at the racetrack, if it does no injustice to others, can be a legitimate form of recreation and appropriate enjoyment. Eating while essential for the survival of the human being, can be a source of exquisite pleasure, enjoyment and, I argue, holiness.

With such a Catholic/Belloc conscience and a healthy stomach, I enjoy and relish (I hope appropriately), eating, especially at eventide, in restaurants of almost any stripe: Italian, Spanish, French, American, Portuguese, Chinese, Irish, Turkish, Moroccan, Mexican and others. Eating in restaurants for me usually is a fulfilling and delightful experience. To be with good friends whose conversation and company I enjoy while savoring fresh, well-prepared food in a charming spot—pampered by waiters, preferably with European accents and manners—suffuses me with a warm and expansive gratitude. Gratitude to whom? That's easy. To the Lord God Himself. Such eating brings me closer to God rather than the opposite.

When I am enjoying a pungent dish of escargots with good friends, I can easily overlook what otherwise might be a source of annoyance (or even uncharity) for me. The guys who eat with their baseball caps on or the screaming babies whose parents seem unconcerned, or the loudmouth who spouts ignorant slurs on my Church, are all ignorable in the flush of my God-given enjoyment. I think this applies even to the hot shot who wears his cap backwards with the peak scratching the nape of his neck. When a glass of red wine courses through my veins, when my friends and I publicly ask God's blessing on our fun and companionship, when I eat good food, when I feel the excitement of open and spirited conversation, my being is drawn to the loving Father, who is God, for providing such bounty to my life. Recently, at a charming Italian restaurant in New York's theatre district, I had a wonderful dinner with a

Catholic family. We laughed and shouted and reached cloud nine. We kidded with the waiters. We drank wine. We ate heartily. We all held hands in a circle and acknowledged Our Lord and Master to the surprise and, I suspect, the envy, of other diners. This was community and the fusion of the spiritual and the material at its best. This was also the Catholicism of which Belloc writes.

It was the heretical Manicheans who saw matter as intrinsically evil, not authentic Catholics. But how many good and intelligent persons have been seduced by this and similar errors! It was so with the great St. Augustine and the brilliant Rene Descartes with his Cartesian split between the spiritual and the material. Both were misled to such a philosophic false extreme.

The Catholic Church has always, as a Church, respected the material. There are innumerable blessings of the physical. Note the blessings for crops, animals, automobiles, marriage beds, airplanes, corpses, and all appropriate[35] material things. We have the blessing *Ad Omnia*—for everything. I consider the great Feast of the Assumption of Our Lady to be a triumphant validation of the material. So holy was her body that the Father did not allow it to decompose. In fact, it is a Catholic belief that all dead bodies will rise again on the last day. How is that for esteeming the physical dimension of us!

The Catholic Church promotes the beautiful with unbelievably gorgeous churches and cathedrals, with music that lifts the soul, with paintings and sculpture, with poetry, and with liturgy which features incense, color, and choreographed movement. All of it uses the physical, the material. While there have been the extremists certainly in other religions who despise matter and who lust to destroy religious art, we have had some misled Catholics who have ranted also in Christ's own Church. We have this periodic rise of Catholic extremists who shout for getting back to basics while grimly missing the warmth and richness of Belloc's Catholicism.

I remember an analogous reference to extremism by William Langland in his work *Piers Plowman* when he wrote of certain Jansenist nuns who "are pure as angels but proud as devils." Clearly, imbalance is always a danger in the spiritual and emotional life. Chastity is a jewel for loving God and, at the same time, highly congenial, not antithetical, to appropriate enjoyment in life.

I recall the wonderful book, *Keys of the Kingdom* (Back Bay Books 1984) by the Scottish physician author, A.J. Cronin. The central character, Fr. Andrew Chisolm, enthuses with his little nephew about the beautiful bounty of God in filling the lake with so many fishes for people to enjoy eating. It does appear that regardless of extreme vegetarian stances, it is the will of the Great God that we should be delighted with dover sole, red snapper and Irish salmon. Who would dare dispute with Jesus who, as God, cooked fish for his followers obviously encouraging others to do likewise?

I certainly won't but I fully intend to enthuse about my Lord. I will sing His praises and thank Him now and hopefully for all eternity. I will continue to link my pollo scarparliello with my faith while I trumpet the Catholic insight about matter. Viva Belloc and his notion of "wherever the Catholic sun doth shine."

On the Nature of Denial and the War on Terror

On the Morning of August 10, 2006, America awoke to the terrifying news that twenty-one Islamic terrorists were arrested in Britain for a near successful attempt to blowup—in mid-air—at least five, possibly ten commercial planes, headed for the United States. Due to the collective expertise of British, American and Pakistani intel, the plot was thwarted, thereby saving almost 5,000 lives. Clearly, the primary credit for this remarkable breakthrough belongs to the United Kingdom whose security is not stifled by the drum beating of ACLU and Hollywood types. Apparently, British pro-active behavior stems from a more realistic understanding of the nature of terrorism as well as a more flexible legal system which allows keepers of the peace to move on a legitimate suspicion.

Only a few days prior, the American public had been bombarded by liberal criticism of the extreme measures taken by the American government (and certainly by the Israelis) in their drive to protect their own people from terrorism. Alleged civil rights violations into telephone privacy were cited as reasons why the American government should not monitor incoming cell phone messages from known terrorists. At the same time, leaks allegedly had been made available through *The New York Times* and CBS to alert the terrorists about American monitoring which fact they did not know previously, thus crippling some aspects of our own homeland security. We heard the old saws: "the public has a right to know," "we have nothing to fear over here from the Islamic extremists," and the usual self-justifications.

Some extreme leftists argue that all the military activity is basically unnecessary, and that international diplomacy and talk (especially at the UN) would solve our modern problems. There is little mention of the relatively unsuccessful and weak UN record (e.g., Rwanda, Sudan, Somalia, etc.). Some of these extremists charge that the United States is responsible for the world's woes, and, by extension, particularly George Bush who was blamed by one such extremist for Katrina since he didn't use his omnipotence over weather. Some elected politicians now urge a cut and run policy in Iraq, believing that America can just leave it all to them and that we should just take care of ourselves. Somehow, they imply, it will all turn out all right.

The suggestion is now being made that the real resolution to terrorism is understanding those who wish us harm. All would be well, we are told, if we (read Americans) would try to understand the Islamic frame of mind. Understanding and love would solve all problems. The day after 9/11, I was confronted by an elderly swimming acquaintance with the assertion that such behavior could have been averted "if only we understand where they are coming from." I suggested that the same understanding should have been applied also to the Nazi Holocaust era. We should try to understand the Nazi drive to exterminate Jews, priests, and gypsies. Since the person in question was Jewish, the dialogue ended abruptly.

Perhaps, it is a convenient and selective memory loss for the Hanoi Janes, the Barbara Striesands, Michael Moores, Alec Baldwins and the like who seem to be unaware (or don't care) of what has happened historically. Most of us can recall 1983 with the more than 200 Marines murdered, the USS Cole, the Twin Tower Bombing of 1993, bombings of American embassies around the world, 9/11 itself! All of these occurred before we entered Iraq. What does it take for the left (liberals?) to understand that there is a real and present danger to the United States? Even this recent concrete example of 8/10/06 seems not to have penetrated the naïve defenses of the liberal mind. Recently, a near senile, retired television interviewer came out of his retirement to interview the president of Iran whose oft stated intent is to annihilate Israel.[36] The liberal old timer came back to the United States to laud his host's virtues and was apparently totally unaware that he had been used for propaganda purposes. He really thought he was acting as a responsible journalist.

The brutally honest documentary *Obsession - Radical Islam's War Against the West*[37] (which surprisingly is not making it to the usual networks) graphically shows that the intent of these people is to destroy us. It is their highest religious value to destroy Americans and their way of life. To suggest to terrorists that they might settle for a lesser goal is impossible for them to accept. It would be totally irreligious for them as would it be for Catholics to give up belief in the Eucharist and the divinity of Christ. This is why some serious scholars privately say that negotiation is a waste of time. While those of us who lived through the World War II era are acutely aware that war is indeed hell, we also know that sometimes it is tragically necessary. Of course, it is public knowledge that Catholics value life as a primary base. It is clear that Pope John Paul II urged us not to go to war with Iraq. Yet, as Scripture tells us, there is a time for war. (Eccles. 3"8)

Sometimes and rarely, a war can be justified. Is a stated and serious threat to national survival sufficient grounds to take up arms? Is America in mortal danger? Are we justified in using our military might? Despite Catholic revulsion to killing it is interesting to note that in the 16th century a Christian coalition led by the papacy went to war to drive back a Turkish (Islamic) attempt to invade Europe. My Jewish forbears were fierce warriors and Moses was a spectacular military leader. Jewish ethos reverberates with Psalm 144 with its opening lines: "Blessed is the Lord, my Rock, who trains my arms for battle and who prepares my hands for war." Spiritual warfare, truly, but also physical warfare to protect God's people from their enemies. Against such a background I find it a bit amusing to observe radical peaceniks engage in cover-up tap dancing to somehow obscure biblical and religious history.

In our contemporary world, is Hollywood, for example, really such a la-la land that fantasy and illusion replace reality? After listening to some outbursts from the left coast, I had a flashback to my South African days when the locals would describe some nut job as being out in the sun too long. It strikes me that these child-flower type people live in a kind of quasi-psychosis. Hopefully Truman Capote's remark made in jest that for every year one spends in California, he loses one point off his IQ, is mere witticism. Perhaps the west coast liberals are living in a naïve fantasy world where they believe that they are protected from evil by the huge Pacific Ocean on the one side and the vast continental mass on the other. Farms, prairies, mountains cannot really protect the glamorous ones from fanatical terrorists. Vigilance, courageous diplomacy, and military deterrence represent our best hope not only to protect our own people (including the juvenile-minded stars of the movies), but also for a whole world. Appeasement and denial inevitably fail.

This is why students of the mind will point out to us the existence of a contemporary, massive denial of reality. The most primitive defense of the mind against what is perceived as a threat is called denial. Many of us have observed this defense in the case of the alcoholic who constantly denies to himself that there is a problem with his drinking. How often I have heard my alcoholic clients slur out remarks which clearly express denial. "I can handle it." "I can stop any time I want." "I only drink socially." "I need a drink to pick me up/reward me." "I'm okay I can drive quite well."

Denial takes many forms one of which is the widespread denial of death. Handling the end of one's life requires some kind of resolution. Some refuse to believe that they will die like everyone else. Some say, in bereavement, "He didn't really die. I pretend that he is coming in tonight as he always did." Funeral directors understand this in their skillful "cosmetizing" of death. Substantive denial is the behavior of the infant. "Make it go away." "Make it all right." Perhaps to face reality absolutely would be catastrophic for anyone. Perhaps we all do need some minimal blunting of the factual in order to survive. Yet, as a rule facing reality is ultimately easier than hoping that the fearful and troublesome and unpleasant and terrifying will somehow disappear in the manner of the infant. The alcoholic who drinks himself senseless in the face of a serious problem will still have to face that problem when his head clears the next day. It just doesn't go away.

The Israeli/Hezbollah conflict is an interesting example. It is uncomfortable to admit to oneself that there are truly evil people in the world. Or even that evil exists at all. The terrorists intentionally aimed their rockets at civilian populations since they believe that this will break the will of the nation. They have no feeling for the old, ill and children. Nothing matters except to destroy. This is evil. At the same time, they will embed themselves within the civilian population, fire their rockets and rely on the reluctance of the Israeli military to do collateral damage. The Israelis will inform the area beforehand that it is about to be attacked. They give sufficient time for non-combatants to leave the area. There is a clear distinction between the two approaches. The liberal mind will for some reason see the Israeli approach as unfair while the terrorists are just oppressed people seeking justice.

Basically, the movement to bring the boys home really is putting one's hands over one's eyes and hoping that it will all go away. Maybe they will leave us alone and maybe they won't fly planes into our buildings anymore. Again denial. The reality is that there is a fundamental conflict between cultures and ideologies. This age-old conflict has erupted, in fact, into a war. This is so uncomfortable to contemplate that the deniers will just try to wish it away. But it just won't go away. In the 1930's, the terrible fear of war moved good people to deny its possibility The memory of the slaughters of World War I with its Verdun and Marne and Argonne was still too raw. But it led world leaders into an unbelievable denial of real danger. Naively, leaders assured their people that we have peace in our time. Such denial led to the most terrible war in human history. Denial won't make peace with terrorists. Only reality orientation will.

The Accused Priest: Victimizer or Victim?

Of all the groups in public life, accusations against the Catholic priest get heavier media attention, wider public discussion and immediate rush to judgment of guilt, than any comparable group in the United States. Public school teachers who are accused ten times more often of sexual molestation than priests of the Archdiocese of New York, politicians who abet crime and dip into the public till, celebrities of the entertainment world who flaunt basic indecencies—almost all, for the most part, are excused with benign, bemused, understanding slaps on the wrist. The big liberal newspapers and television outlets do note these indiscretions but situate them in a relatively obscure spot in the dissemination of the news. Non-priest negatives are allowed to dissipate while priests' failings, actual or otherwise, are quickly, almost gleefully, fueled.

One can wonder whether the eagerness to destroy a priest is really an intent to destroy the Catholic Church. The most pivotal point of the Catholic Church is the priesthood and hence can become the target area for non-objective and agenda driven reporting. One notes that clergymen of other denominations who, though married, have proportionally equal sexual failure rates, are not highlighted the way Catholic priests are. Why is this? Is it that these priests, as special and public articulators of God's holiness, should be held to a higher moral standard than politicians, teachers, rock singers and even other clergymen? Perhaps, so! But is that the whole story?

Is all this true? Is this paranoia on the part of Catholics? Is this mere hypersensitivity? Dr. Philip Jenkins of Penn State University wrote a formidable book, *The New Anti-Catholicism: The Last Acceptable Prejudice* (Oxford University Press 2003), exposing the reality of the powerful prejudice behind the movement to discredit Catholicism. Tammy Bruce, a fair-minded, lesbian author and media personality, exposes much of the force behind what we are calling unfairness in her unsettling book, *The Death of Right and Wrong* (Prima Lifestyles 2003). Why is this? Why is there such a volcanic reaction to alleged misconduct of a priest? There are surely many possible motivational dynamics behind the attacks on priests. Some have more cogency and truth than others but all should be examined.

First, the allegations might be true. If this is so, then, we congratulate the media. It is crucial that not only our children but our youth be protected from vicious destructive adults of any and all professions. We enthuse that a wayward priest is immediately dismissed and punished like any other criminal. The Church benefits from such a move as do all Catholic members and most especially do the male teenage members who will then be protected from that priest with his (statistically probable) same-sex compulsions.[38] It is alleged that all the media is doing is to contribute to a healthier and more honest society. While this sounds plausible (and probably is, in the case of unfaithful priests), the implied universal judgment of guilt and suspicion applied to all priests is clearly unfair and untrue. It simply isn't so. All studies rate the sexual failure rate in the priesthood as an average around 3 percent. Over sixty years this becomes devastating, but it must be seen in perspective.[39]

Unless one wears intellectual blinders of ignorance or prejudice, there is clear and authenticated evidence of anti-Catholic animus. Bluntly stated, sheer prejudice and dislike of the Catholic Church may be driving editors, publishers, journalists, anchor persons and educators to such unmitigated slanted reporting. Clearly, there is always the possibility that these driven zealots might be only unconsciously bigoted. They, when challenged, indignantly insist that they are only telling the public what the public needs[40] to know with all the frills one learns in the liberal Columbia School of Journalism. However, we have witnessed somewhat startling revelations from courageous reporters who tell the truth about the media from the inside. Bernie Goldberg, a long-time reporter from CBS wrote two shocking books about what really happens in newsrooms. In his number one *New York Times* bestseller, *Bias: A CBS Insider Exposes How the Media Distort the News* (Regnery Publishing 2001), he created a national firestorm when he exposed the biases of the mainstream media. His second book, *Arrogance: Rescuing America from the Media Elite* (Grand Central Publishing 2003), tells of the assumptions of media which lead to biased reporting and slanted news. Objective news reporting seems far away from today's reality. One must consider the agenda which begin to become obvious.

The article in *America* (Sept. 25, 2006) by Monica Applewhite of Praesidium, Inc. called "Putting Abuse in Context" gives an interesting perspective. The problem of sexual abuse occurs in a much wider context than one can glean from the standard press reports. It occurs far more frequently than the homosexual Catholic priest scandal. She presents tested data through which guidelines for dealing with sexual offenders have been clearly articulated. However, these guidelines are presented for every situation—not only the Catholic Church. Boy Scouts, Big Brothers, YMCA, the Episcopal Church among others have all acted appropriately in incorporating guidelines into their structures. Percentagewise, there is not a great deal of difference relative to failure rates. However, all should be treated equally, and there ought to be a level playing field here. Why accent one over any other?

One possibility for the agenda focusing on Catholic priests might stem from the contemporary insistence on what is called sexual rights. This insistence usually means that the modern wishes to separate sexual activity from the possibility of procreating a child. This position is obvious when one dialogues with that segment of our society jocosely called "the Second Avenue bar crowd" where boy meets girl after a hard day's work with implication of fun and games. The witness of chastity in Catholic priests and religious is largely maintained as advertised but does evoke criticism from the moderns who loudly proclaim that chastity (or celibacy as they see it) is impossible to achieve. Therefore, those who live allegedly chaste lives are either lying or are very sick.[41] So when an accusation against a priest is made, shouts of triumph and exaltation make the headlines. It is as if sexual weakness in the homosexual priest validates the free lifestyle of the critics. This point simply suggests that the chastity of priests is a rebuke to the champions of the new way of life.

There is always the possibility that the critics were offended by some arrogant Pastor of their childhood, and they have never gotten over it. But who of us was not slighted or pushed around or belted by a parochial schoolteacher? Is destroying a religious life by calumny[42] justified?[43] It is for no small reason that the Eighth Commandment from God states: "Thou shalt not bear false witness against thy neighbor." In effect, this is what the Church labels a mortal sin objectively greasing the slide into an eternal hell.

A case in point is a recent situation where an elderly priest, suffering from cancer, has been accused by someone that this priest molested him[44] almost fifty years ago. The priest was notified that he cannot function as a priest publicly unless and until the charge is fully examined. The priest was given no further information. The priest, totally stunned, thought this was a practical joke. He asked when did this allegedly happen? The reply: "We are not sure." He asked where did this allegedly happen? The reply: "We are not sure." He asked how often did this allegedly happen? The reply: "We are not sure." He asked what was the nature of the alleged offense? The reply: "We are not sure." Who is the accuser? Reply: "Someone."

In effect, without any proof, authorities acted completely on the word of someone, who suddenly surfaces to defame a priest with an honorable career in the priesthood. The priest, well known by many colleagues (including this writer for fifty years), has no inclination or interest in homosexual matters, has clear devotion to the Lord and Our Lady and has been rightfully trusted by anyone who has crossed his priestly path. One must ask again the hard questions. Why would anyone engage in such despicable, unrighteous behavior?

For the streetwise, of course, the first thought is money. In my own experience of serving for five years on a diocesan committee for reviewing clerical sexual misconduct, I have seen several flimsy allegations from money-seeking people. Unwisely, sometimes Church authorities tried to buy off accusers with what really amounted to hush money. The obvious occurred. The accuser asked for (or pleaded for) more money in the light of the rising cost of living (or unanticipated expenses). Interestingly, in the initial stage of accusation, the accuser would often pointedly state that, "I am not interested in money—only in justice and protection of others from this priest." However, in a surprisingly short period of time, somehow, the matter of money crept into the investigation. Subtly, quietly, suddenly we are talking about significant sums of money.

One lawyer, interested in this sphere of practice, noted during the height of the scandal that a "lot money can be made off the Church." Another, in the state of New Jersey, who specializes in suing the Catholic Church notes that he needs only one or two such cases per year to live very comfortably. One person who was molested by both a priest and a public-school teacher said that he would sue the priest over the teacher because there was more money to be made from the Church than the Board of Ed. One cannot easily dismiss this factor in probing for the truth of this whole problem. However, it is not the only or even dominant factor involved.

It is also most interesting that when an American bishop announced that his diocese would not dole out large cash palliatives to persons allegedly molested by priests. Henceforth, he said that all accusations will go to trial. No concessions. No settlements. Court trials only. How does one then explain the sudden plummeting and decline of accusations after his announcement. Is it cynical or realistic to note that dollar signs are flashing in greedy eyes?

The infamous Tawana Brawley case of some years ago was a glaring example of calumny and its heartbreaking consequences for so many persons falsely accused. Broken marriages, bankruptcies, emotional breakdowns, came on the heels of an absurd charge which was encouraged and supported by prominent persons. At present (Jan. 2007) there is possibly another glaring case of false accusation in the Duke University lacrosse situation wherein several young men have been accused of sexual molestation. These young men may be innocent but have suffered enormous losses of time, money, and reputation. These are not examples of persecuting the Catholic Church but they do illustrate the evil of false accusations.

In the Catholic experience there is the notorious case of Cardinal Bernadin of Chicago in which a homosexual man claimed through the dubious mode of dream recall[45] that Bernadin molested him years before. The man recanted his claim and the Cardinal was totally exonerated. His Eminence, however, did publicly reveal the suffering he endured from this falsehood as he was dying from cancer. Was this man's accusation for the hope of money? Was it to embarrass the Catholics for the Church's stance on the evil of homosexual behavior? Was he encouraged by activist gay groups in their campaign to break down basic morals, as has been suggested?

Is it possible that the accuser mis-identifies? Is he a psychotic ranting against some demon in his fantasy life which torments his psyche? Is he just hopping on the Catholic bashing band wagon? Any of these possibilities is preferable to the sheer evil of a deliberate false accusation. Whatever the reality, the innocent priest is a victim. The guilty priest is obviously another story. Telling the truth wherever it may lead is still the way to go. The Scriptures clearly teach that the truth does make one free. However, lies and calumnies have a way of catching up. Beware, ye ones who wish evil on innocents!

Should Religious Personnel Wear
Distinctive Garb?

One sunny Sunday morning I routinely announced to a crowded church that nuns would be collecting money after Mass for the foreign missions, a rather common pious practice among Catholics. I also announced, whether through innocence or unconscious intent, that they would be wearing religious habits. There was an instant, spontaneous, huge applause which I immediately judged to be linked to my mention of how the nuns were dressed. After Mass, an irate woman, somewhat elderly but stylishly dressed, charged me with belligerent flashing eyes and a fierce challenge. "Religious habits don't make the nun!" She declared energetically that she, too, was a nun, just as sincerely dedicated to God and good works as these habited collectors. And couldn't I see the little cross pinned to the lapel of her designer jacket, indicating her total self-donation? Once she brought my attention to it, I was able to see it as a religious symbol.

Of course, I meekly suggested that the applause probably meant that Catholic laity liked seeing their religious leaders in distinctive garb but that I was sure that this angry lady was a very good and effective person. But her reaction does cause one to ponder on such a situation. What does one make of it? Clearly, the wearing of distinctive and immediately recognizable religious garb has fallen into considerable disfavor. Priests rarely wear clerical collars, partly because of the social stress of the homosexual-priest scandal and partly for personal secular motivation.[46] Religious brothers, of my world, have almost entirely forsaken religious garb even in the classroom. Nuns who wear traditional habits are viewed in some quarters as obscurantist and throwbacks. Recently one such nun told me of some city workers called into the convent to correct a water defect. The workers asked the sisters: "Why are you dressed like that'?" "No one dresses like that anymore." And on and on.

What does all this mean? Does it correlate with other unhappy Catholic experiences? Perhaps not at all. Yet many social commentators say that there could be a partial link (or meaning) between the discarding of religious garb and the collapse of Catholic vigor. Is moving to secular garb merely a symptom indicating something far deeper? Is it just an effect hinting at a more corrosive cause? Does the secular move to discard religious garb by Catholic leaders influence the Catholic laity to cut religious corners of the Catholic faith? It deserves investigation.

I suggest that there are some assessments we can safely accept. Let me give one example which can possibly be extrapolated into a wider context. Shortly after the 9/11 horror of 2001, there was a call for national prayer by which the American people would call upon the help of the Almighty. In fact, churches were crammed with people seeking consolation and understanding by huddling together before God. At our own church of St. Paul the Apostle, the priests stood at the church doors and were almost mobbed by people needing to verbalize their fears and puzzlements to someone they considered to be close to the Lord. However, one of the priests who believes that priests should dress in secular garb stood alone at the door—I think somewhat forlornly. He hungered to be consulted as a priest but no one approached him. He wore a classy business suit believing this would make him more approachable as a priest. But sadly for him, the people saw him as one of them. In times like 9/11, they wanted someone not like them. His idea that his secular dress would make him more accessible and attractive to laity worked exactly in the opposite direction. They ignored him. Not intentionally but only because they had no way of knowing that he was a priest.

It was almost laughable (at least comedic) that at the next Mass that day our secular minded priest shows up—not in the business suit—but in a traditional black suit with clerical collar. Is he now being pragmatic, ruthlessly forsaking his beloved New-Age kind of style? Or is it humility? Or hypocrisy? Or what? All we do know is that the laity (at that time) wanted their priests dressed as priests not as bankers or sports heroes. But perhaps the more salient factor to be probed is the possible link between discarding religious garb and the contemporary spiritual malaise.

I have visited convents where the nuns wore short shorts, tight t-shirts, smoked, drank martinis and spoke droolingly of how edenic sex must be. This type of modern (though graying) nun is usually of the ultra-feminist coloration, who often expresses cautious and ambiguous support of artificial contraception and same-sex marriage. She is strikingly anti-clerical and highly critical even of Pope John Paul II. She puzzles and dismays me. It is also interesting that religious orders such as these are dying on the vine from a lack of recruits. Many of the single Catholic young women of my world who are daily communicants and who have great love of the Lord show utterly no interest in joining these liberated religious groups. One mentioned to me that these religious live no differently than does she. Why should she join such worldly, jaded groups? Ironically, this may ultimately prove to be a blessing rather than a tragedy because there is surfacing a most fascinating religious or cultural phenomenon which well may mean a true revival of religious life. We are seeing the new nun.

The liberal magazine *Time* featured an article, "Today's Nun Has a Veil" (Nov. 20, 2006), on the surprising growth of new and more orthodox religious orders appearing throughout this country. The sub-title "More young women are entering convents. How they are changing the sisterhood," implies a great deal. These women are mostly in their twenties and thirties usually career types seeking more meaning in their lives (and are sometimes empty nest moms). Most of them have not been blighted by the wild adolescent binges we saw in the post-Vatican II period but have been invigorated by the charismatic appeal of Pope John Paul II and his interpretation of modern feminism as a way for women to express Christian values. This is the JP2 generation.

It is most interesting to note that these enthusiastic, vigorous, educated young women want a structured life centering around the Eucharist and community prayer. They value the daily Mass. They respect the priesthood (even knowing that some priests are rebels, nerds or unfaithful). They are loyal to the teaching of the Church which is called the Magisterium. They are sincere about the evangelical counsels. They profess their primary commitment to Jesus through vows of poverty, chastity and obedience. And they mean it! They truly believe that they are making a radical statement cutting through the murky disorientation which confuses our today society. Their counterculture announcement is embodied by the wearing of the veil. One young nun quoted in the *Time* article says, "It's a trend with younger women wanting to wear the veil now." And, besides, they laugh a lot, exude an unmistakable joyful spirit, roller blade and ride bikes through traffic and parks. It is also noteworthy that these new communities usually wear full habits, ankle length.

It has been my unbelievable good fortune to have been the confessor for a convent of the Sisters of Life for five years. I have met the new nun close up. She is a talented, normal, vibrant young woman who makes a choice, even if culturally radical, to give her life to Jesus Christ. She is not the mythical broken-hearted damsel or the one who can't do anything else. She is a doctor, former Air Force nurse (Captain), psychologist, computer programmer, geologic engineer, teacher, former Marine, ex-professional opera singer, political scientist, blogger.

This particular group, Sisters of Life, is a relative newcomer with a mere fifteen years of existence. Yet it numbers over fifty members with prospects of many more. Its apostolate is specific. It deals with young women who reject abortion in favor of life and with any kind of attack on the sacredness of human life. Other similar groups throughout this country are experiencing even more rapid growth such as the Dominican sisters of Mary (in Ann Arbor), which, founded in 1997, already has seventy-three members. Their average age, incidentally, is twenty-four! So I tentatively suggest that there is a correlation between religious garb and active, lively Catholicism (exemplified as entering religious life), regardless of the furious insistence that the relaxed lifestyle of the dying communities is in sync with a vigorous religious Life. Somehow, once the religious casts off the habit or the collar, irreligious behavior often follows. The hypothetical correlation needs to be deeply studied for an objective understanding of what has happened in the last forty years.[47]

It is further grist for the correlation mill that male communities are experiencing the same kind of phenomenon. The most striking one in my experience is that founded approximately twenty years ago by the brilliant and saintly Fr. Benedict Groeschel and his eight companions who left a very large order because of serious differences on fundamentals.[48] These new religious, called The Franciscan Friars of the Renewal (CFRs), wear a distinctive gray friar's habit complete with cowl, sandals and beard. They sleep on the floor, cook all their meals, do all their own housework and live a true community life. They wear their habits on the street, on airplanes, subways, busses, anywhere they go. They are highly visible. They insist that they make public statements by their manner of dress, namely that they believe in Catholicism. On entering any chapel or church wherein the Blessed Eucharist is reserved, they unapologetically kneel and kiss the floor as a public act of faith. They are fiercely loyal to Jesus, the Catholic Church and the Magisterium.

Is it surprising that their recruit numbers are astonishingly high in this alienated me-first era? They are beginning to get fifteen to twenty young people each year, attracted by the clarity of dedication and the holiness of the friars. Their retention rate is good and they now number over one hundred members. Like the young nun candidates, these potential friars are looking for some sense of meaning to their lives and seem to be attracted to a life which challenges limits of their generosity.

There is a hypothesis here which, while needing research and considerable analyzable data, can be stated in research terms. Does the wearing of a habit coupled with a focused apostolate correlate positively with high recruitment? Does secular garb coupled with diffuse apostolates correlate negatively with low recruitment?

For further input of data, I offer the following. I have been further blessed to have been Professor of Human Sexuality and Counseling at two major seminaries for a total of thirty-one years. Over the years I have noted the clear movement toward a more traditional approach to priesthood in the Catholic Church. There seems to be a more open expression of piety and rejection of the semi-diluted theological climate of the late 20th century. It strikes me that young priests who are clerically attired, are praying more than their middle-aged, somewhat angst-driven confreres who like to dress in Levis and sport shirts. Further, it is becoming a common observation in the priest community that the young priests are markedly more open in their loyalty to the Holy Father and less likely to have the theological hang-ups of their predecessors. Is there some kind of link here? Does wearing clericals indicate a more, if unconscious, commitment to priesthood?

In my last teaching years at Dunwoodie Seminary of Yonkers, a group of students began meeting quietly each afternoon at five for an hour of adoration before the Blessed Sacrament. The numbers increased until almost the whole student body was present at this optional devotion. A salient point of this observation is that all the students were dressed either in soutanes (cassocks) or in clerical collar. A further point is the obvious and pervasive devotion to the Catholic ethos in that theologate. Again, is there some kind of link here?

So many Catholic lay persons have expressed their pleasure at seeing their religious leaders dressed like Catholic religious leaders. They know that the religious habit or collar almost shrieks out in the secular marketplace that God matters. So does the average religious who has probably experienced the hostile stare or obscene remark from those who are rebuked by the religious garb. But he also knows the friendly smile and friendly support from so many more. Beyond the effect on others, wearing religious garb reminds the religious himself/herself of the commitment one has made to God. Unbelievably, this is easy to overlook in this very secular environment. Wearing religious garb is a protection as well as a proclamation. Let us hope that the trend continues and that it might even break through the distortions of the stiff-necked earlier generation. (And I am eighty-five!)

The Catholic Church Vigorously Supports
Stem Cell Research and Treatment

In the framework of Catholic thinking, the Fifth Commandment (Thou shalt not kill) requires explicit protection of human life from the moment of conception until actual physical death. Also, by a series of penumbras and emanations, a sensitive Catholic conscience includes (under that commandment) the need of good diet, exercise, appropriate recreation, regular check-ups, avoidance of unnecessary risks to life and limb[49] and good medical research. Such a conscience is highly compatible with, and indeed necessary for a sophisticated spiritual life. Indeed, real Catholicism and real science make congenial bedfellows. Within recent history, Pope John Paul II worked strenuously to exploit the resources of reason and science to enhance a Catholic understanding of how God works. More recently, for example, the Archbishop of Melbourne, Australia, Cardinal George Pell, offered $150,000 in grants for research into adult stem cells as a concrete commitment to morally licit scientific innovation.

Such an offer reflects an accurate picture of the Catholic Church and its vigorous support for the remarkable work done with stem cell so far. There have been some strikingly successful treatments, using stem cells, for spinal cord injuries, leukemia, Krabbe's Leukodystrophy (a rare degenerative enzyme disorder) Parkinson's disease and several others. The stem cells derived were from various sources. Sometimes, from pregnancy related tissues like umbilical cords, placentas and amniotic fluid. Other times, from bone marrow, livers, epidermis, retinas, skeletal tissues, intestine, brain, dental pulp. Some clinicians are using fat from liposuction for significant numbers of adult type stem cells. Some have used neural stem cells from cadavers as late as twenty hours after death.

Clearly, such medical breakthroughs are very exciting inasmuch as stem cells can potentially be used to replace and heal damaged tissue in the body in a manner previously unknown. The enthusiasm for such research has rightly reached a very high level of expectation—almost as if, in the future, one might have a repair kit in the medicine cabinet ready for any medical emergency. However, as is the case in things human and scientific, one must exercise some caution, step back for a moment, and examine what we are saying. There are possibly some catches in the case. And there are some very real negatives which must also be examined.

The above rosy assessment focuses on adult stem cells or miscarriages. It does not accept what amounts to the baby-killing mode of obtaining stem cells. But even with the inclusion of the miscarriage possibility, it does appear that adult cells are preferable to embryonic stem cells. There are huge reasons why adult cells are preferable. They naturally exist in our bodies in the microenvironment of an adult body as natural repair mechanisms for many of our physical ills. They fit. Whereas, when we introduce embryonic stem cells into an adult microenvironment, something seriously negative can happen. Scientific caution is necessary here. With the use of embryonic stem cells, teratomas (or tumors) can develop which cannot easily be controlled. Immune system reactions can occur. These cannot be sloughed off as minor points. If transplanted cells are attacked by the immune system, the entire tissue will be the target of what can be a disastrous attack. This is the tissue in which the foreign cell resides (i.e., embryonic cell in adult microenvironment).

Dr. Maureen L. Condic, professor of neurobiology (University of Utah, School of Medicine) in an article appearing in *First Things*, Jan. 2007, questions the whole notion of embryonic stem cell research. She notes that since 2002 (NIH database) there have been more than eight highly funded research projects investigating human embryonic stem cells. In 2006, NIH anticipated spending was "just $24,3000,000."[50] There have been 900 research papers submitted since 2002 plus an additional 1,000 plus papers investigating animal research. Dr. Condic wrote in 2002: "[T]here is no compelling scientific argument f or the public support of research on human embryos." She informs her readers that scientists define serious scientific challenges as problems that have stubbornly resisted the best attempts of science to solve them. After thirty years of billions of dollars spent and countless hours of research with no results, immune rejection and tumor formation are still serious scientific and medical challenges. What has come of all the futile research? Using the line of Ron McKay of NIH (relative to the admitted studied ambiguities of some lobbyists[51]) which states that "[P]eople need a fairy tale," Dr. Condic asks her definitive question. "Isn't it time Americans recognize the promise of obtaining medical miracles from embryonic stem cells for the fairy tale it really is?"

Dr. Tad Pacholczyk, neuroscientist from Yale, Harvard Medical and Massachusetts General Hospital solidifies her point.[52] He states the following: "Adult stem cells have been used successfully in human therapies for many years. But on the other side no therapies in humans have ever been successfully carried out using embryonic stem cells." In the light of this information, it does seem unintelligent and imprudent to cut into the funding for already proven therapies using adult stem cells and redirect the money to an unproven and highly resistant possibility.

Hence, one finds it difficult to understand the ambiguous positions of famous names who drumbeat the virtues of embryonic stem research. Television and radio commercials sometimes feature Hollywood types who plead disingenuously[53] for ESCR (Embryonic stem cell research). This is sometimes done very slickly for funding without ever actually mentioning that human embryos are involved. The trick is to play on human sympathy. Sometimes, it is done most successfully on an uniformed public. It prompts one to ask several questions. What is their real motivation? What is their scientific information? Is it a case of mere ignorance, misplaced compassion or is it agenda? It has also been suggested that there is the possibility of enormous amounts of money to be made. Is this sheer nobility and humanitarianism?

It is particularly surprising in the case of educated alleged practicing Catholics. These persons have at least the information I, and thousands of others, have available. And, additionally, they have the incomparable guidance of the Holy Spirit through His Church. How can it be that the Governor of New Mexico, Bill Richardson (D) is allocating six million dollars in state taxpayer funds not only for the laudable adult stem cell research but also for embryonic stem cell research? The Archbishop and Bishops of New Mexico have urged him to practice Catholic beliefs in his important work. They, in effect, remind him that ESCR is destroying human life. Is his faith of such little import?

The Governor of Colorado, Bill Ritter (D), was similarly challenged (on another level) by Archbishop Chaput of Denver. Ritter plans to fund Planned Parenthood which Ritter says, "specializes in the business of preventing them" (*sic:* children). Perhaps, to these gentlemen, being a Catholic is merely a cultural, social or familial accoutrement, to be kept in some harmless, non-meaningful closet. It does cause one to wonder. Only God knows, of course, but in these turbulent times, we, in the trenches, find such behavior troubling.

But, to the point. Does the Catholic Church support stem cell research? Of course. Catholic concern for the treatment of illness has been legendary throughout the ages. However, as a spiritual and humanitarian leader, it cannot and does not support the barbarism of cloning which, as a procedure, specifically destroys a human embryo in order to extract embryonic stem cells. While there has been an almost fevered race to generate a human clone, there have been only a few reports of alleged human cloning, none of which is verifiable. Some have been clear chicanery promoted by a "quasi-religious group for its own publicity" (Cf. Dr. Condic) The most outrageous was that claimed by a South Korean group (March 2004) led by Hwang Woo-Suk. The miracle has been accomplished. "We have eleven patient-specific stem cells lines from human clones." Immediately, there was a clamor to have the Bush restriction on ESCR removed. However, it was soon discovered that Hwang's miracle was a scientific fraud and that all the claimed cloned stem cell lines were fakes. Dr. Condic assures us that this should be no surprise. It is extremely difficult to clone any animal. Human cloning would be much more difficult than any other.

Even Dolly the sheep must be seen in perspective. Dolly was born as an abnormal. And the only one to survive to live birth out of 277 cloned embryos. How difficult to clone anything! Also, Dolly had to be euthanized due to her poor health. This was not so highly publicized as was her birth.

However, with all of the above said, let us suppose that modern technologies, now available (or soon will be) are able to use embryonic type stem cell without crossing any moral lines. (Note: embryonic type not embryonic stem cells). Suppose those germ cells (which can be derived from the testicles) can be transmuted into embryonic-type stem cells and have the same alleged flexibility claimed for ones derived out of embryos? The Church would have no objection since there is no killing involved here. But we would insist (as with good science) that research be done on animals first.

While we say, yes, Catholicism is highly supportive of stem cell research and its use to alleviate human ills, at the same time we also say that we are highly supportive of the culture of life. We oppose the culture of death, which is inherent in embryonic stem cell research, a highly speculative project.

Yes, I Am a Catholic and I Did Not Vote for John F. Kennedy

After nearly forty-seven years of political observation, I am delighted that I boycotted JFK—even though I came from a tightly knit Catholic ghetto. In 1960, there was an almost cosmic adoration of "Jack" which was sprawling across the nation. He was an idol who drew a huge Catholic vote. However, these voters had no real way of knowing or assessing what his election would mean, not only to Catholicism in this country but also to the spiritual nerve of the nation. By an unconscious peasant instinct of mine, I voted against my whole family's political tradition. I, a Catholic, voted Republican.

I knew that Jack was a very bright, self-assured, handsome, extremely rich young fellow who went to exclusive educational establishments. He played rough and tumble touch football at his family's upper-crust Cape Cod home. He sailed classy yachts off the Massachusetts coast. He was a World War II hero in the South Pacific and had (I thought) a beautiful wife. He was telegenic (which quality would eventually win him the presidency) and was a polished public speaker.

My own little world in the tenement area of Manhattan's west side resounded with the battle cry: "He is Irish and Catholic. How can we not vote for him? We, the downtrodden, despised, undereducated, dumb Irish will be lifted up as a class—once Jack is elected—to great new levels. New respect. New opportunities. New horizons. We can stand very tall. We will have finally really made it. Don't think any further. Just vote for one of our own." Still, I smelled a rat.

We had all heard of the Protestant fear that a Catholic President would trash the First Amendment, establish a Romish state Church and probably have a Vatican ammunition dump in the basement of the White House. There were ten million homes receiving anti-Catholic tracts in 1960. The nine-million-member Southern Baptist Convention, among others, launched big anti-Kennedy campaigns. Protestants were asked to stand up and be counted on Reformation Sunday, October 30, 1960. It recalled for me the bitter, vitriolic anti-Catholic election year when Al Smith, an open and vigorous Catholic, was the Democratic candidate for President. In his case, his Catholicism played a significant but not exclusive part in his defeat to Herbert Hoover. Although I was seven years old, I learned very early about religious discrimination—which was not only anti-Semitic but virulently anti-Catholic. Consequently, despite my discomfort with Jack, I did identify with him to some degree.

However, Colleen Carroll Campbell, a fellow of the Ethics and Public Forum writes in the *Catholic World Report* (Feb. 2007) that Kennedy was anything but a devout and vigorous Catholic like Smith. He had poor catechesis, gave "not a whit for theology," never mentioned any view of man's relationship with God. Cardinal Cushing openly acknowledged that Jack was never very religious. His own wife, Jackie Kennedy, claimed to be mystified by the religious controversy about her husband because she said, "Jack is such a poor Catholic." Episcopalian Bishop Jim Pike saw Jack's position was that of a "thorough going secularist who really believes that a man's religion and his decision-making can be kept in two watertight compartments." Robert McAfee Brown saw JFK as "a rather irregular Christian." Martin Marty, Lutheran theologian, saw him as "spiritually rootless and, politically, almost disturbingly secular."

Although I did not know all this in 1960, I did read his talk at Houston about Church-State Separation on September 12th of that year. Before an audience of several hundred Protestant clergy, he made his case for disavowing the influence of his Catholic Faith on his political choices. Basically, he said.

"I will make my decisions in accordance with what my conscience[54] tells me...and without regard to outside religious pressures...no power or threat of punishment could cause me to decide otherwise...." Campbell writes that many Catholic Bishops feared JFK as President because of his hardline positions against Church policies.

JFK's speechwriter, Ted Sorensen, claimed that the Jesuit priest, Fr. J.C. Murray was a consultant for the composition of the speech. But Campbell claims that Murray disapproved of Jack's strident separationism since the Constitution does not call for a public square "stripped of all religious rhetoric." This stripping is what Fr. R. J. Neuhaus has called "the naked public square." The Constitution does allow politicians and voters to engage in faith-based social activism and to defend their religiously derived principles in that very public square. Yet, JFK made a pledge to expunge all traces of religious influence from his governing decisions.[55] It was interesting to me that at a recent luncheon, a priest-friend, a respected and older Jesuit informed me with great confidence that Murray dictated that speech to JFK over the phone.

In any event, it was that speech that alarmed me and formed my resolve not to back handsome Jack, but holding my nose, to vote instead for tricky Dick. It is only with hindsight that my visceral instinct or psychologist's nose makes sense. Kennedy was, de facto, more of a Deist than Catholic. Though he attended Mass regularly, his Catholicism was more cultural and familial than anything else. His thinking didn't reflect any involvement of God with His creatures. Jack's God kept His distance from them. They were on their own. Once He created them, they were masters of their fates and captains of their souls. Jack said: "Our problems are man-made—therefore they can be solved by man."

Where does one see in his thinking any reference to the fallen world through original sin[56] or reliance on and trust in the power and grace so emphasized in Christian life views?

Those who have followed him politically, have absorbed his separationism and hence have departed from the notion of public religion. When one studies the American beginnings, it is obvious that the Founding Fathers believed in the separation of any established (or particular) church and the state. They did not believe in the separation of religion and state. This is a substantive and essential distinction. Yet, in modern thinking (read: JFK) religion, as such, should be kept out of sight. Perhaps, in the home. Or in the church. Or in one's own soul. But not in public discourse or decision making. Does not this ultimately lead to moral relativism? Such a possibility leads someone like me, a Jew, to become afraid.

We dread that relativism finally means Dachau! This terrorizes me and others like me because then it is consensus that matters, not eternal fixed truth.[57] Yet, this practical relativism (or Kennedy logic) finds a congenial home in the modern American political world (and probably elsewhere). This is appalling to me. But it is even more appalling when it is mouthed by some alleged Catholic politicians. This is particularly appalling because the public debate often touches on core meanings of life, such as embryonic stem cell research, physician assisted suicide, abortion and partial-birth abortion, same-sex marriages—on the very value of life itself. Or at least the Catholic notion of life! To exclude religion from such debate is not only un-American but dumb.

Mario Cuomo, a brilliant speaker and thinker, in a series of tortured intellectual maneuvers set out (using the Kennedy relativistic thinking) to make a case for the pro-choice[58] Catholic politicians. New York's Cardinal, John Joseph O'Connor, himself extremely bright and political science literate, had bluntly stated that he did not believe a Catholic in good conscience could support legal abortion. His statement created a huge turbulence in the world of politics. Geraldine Ferraro, the defeated candidate for the vice presidency (a declared Catholic as well as a pro-choice or pro-abortion supporter) was, in my opinion, furious with the then archbishop who was doing nothing more than his basic job in pointing out the evil of complicity.

Cuomo stipulated in a startling speech at Notre Dame University, twenty-four years after Kennedy's Houston speech, that there are "no final truths." I, personally, became very disappointed in Cuomo—particularly with this statement. He had written in his *Diaries* (Random House 1984) how much he valued his soul more than anything else. He wrote how much he admired St. Thomas More who stood against the government when it was against his faith. More who was prepared to be decapitated rather than compromise his Catholic conscience. This was the More who said: "I love my king but I love my God even more."

In my disappointment, I felt that Cuomo, instead of loyalty to God, used the Kennedy bifurcation to trumpet what to me was one of the more intellectually insulting stances of modern times. He argued that not only are Catholics not betraying their consciences by supporting abortion, but they are, in accord with good American tradition, not imposing their view on anyone else.[59] This has a kind of patriotic tinge to it.[60] This can be done, he said, in effect, by interiorly holding that abortion is intrinsically evil but exteriorly supporting those who wish legally to abort babies. This could apply similarly to the barbarism of partial birth abortion. In effect, there is ultimately no moral principle which can determine or effect what our political conduct should be.

Cuomo incorrectly used the Bernardin schema of seamless garment as background insisting that abortion is just a single issue among many and has "no preemptive significance." This would surprise our Pope who, in 2004, as Cardinal Ratzinger, clearly points out that abortion has greater moral weight than war and capital punishment in which there is much room for dialogue. With an abortion there is none. Further, Cuomo argues that government should simply carry out the will of the people Therefore, if the will of the people is for abortion, it should be done. On consensus. The interior belief of the government leader is, in a sense, irrelevant.

However, I was deeply disappointed with my fallen hero when Mario, in effect, says that it is legitimate to try to influence or even impose in other issues except abortion. Some concept of consensus. It becomes most confusing when I recall that Governor Cuomo used his power of veto against a strong popular desire to reinstate the death penalty. His veto was a function of his personal disagreement with the essence of capital punishment.

It seems to me that contradiction is woven into these positions. In 2004, John Kerry had a 100% voting score from the National Abortion Rights Action League which he defended based on his Catholic conscience defined, he says, by Pius XXIII (who never existed) and Paul VI in his Vatican Council. Paul did not convene the Council. John did. Following his poorly-formed conscience is no way to be a good Catholic.

There are American bishops who bravely point out, regardless of political pressures, that social leaders who knowingly depart from Catholic Church teaching pay a price. By scandalizing the church-going faithful in such a public way, they forfeit their right to receive the Eucharist. Archbishop Raymond Burke of St. Louis, for example, incurred the wrath of liberal personalities, including some Catholic religious for such brazen statements. He has been called ineffectual in his position implying, apparently, that silence in the face of evil is a better course to follow. Yet the tolerant stance seems demographically to do nothing but reinforce the slide away from the practice of the Catholic faith. Can some of contemporary lukewarmness of certain Catholics be linked to this style?

Yet as inexplicable as is the bifurcation stance in laity, the twist in the minds of clergy is even more astounding. One of the worst appears to be the Jesuit ex-Congressman (D. Mass.) Robert Drinan. His fellow congressman, Robert Dornan, himself a spiritual/religious/political storm center, wrote "I fear for his immortal soul." Fr. Drinan was a strong advocate of abortion campaigns who approved of President Clinton's veto on the partial-birth abortion ban. We learn that Drinan appeared as a character witness for Clinton during the impeachment hearings, advised pro-abortion John Kerry during the 2004 election year and turned a Mass in January 2007 into anti American politics. He called the amendment to ban Federal funds for abortion "uncharitable." Fortunately, he was forced to leave politics by the Pope himself. But, more sadly, how could this happen to a priest of God? Sexual molestations by priests are bad enough, even if done from weakness or psychological distortion. But Drinan was an intellectual and his plans were calculated and thought out, and much more evil in the long run. Again, is there some kind of linkage with the thought of John F. Kennedy?

The present Speaker of the House, Nancy Pelosi, is the ultimate (hyperbolically predictable) outcome. Dornan calls her "maybe the most dangerous leader in the long campaign by anti-Catholics within the Church who mislead Americans, get elected and advance the culture of death."[61] In a personal conversation with her in which Dornan urged her to follow the Church's teaching, she replied (with a laugh): "Oh, come on, Bob. What would you do if one of your daughters was raped by a black man?" Does racism justify slaughter of little human fetuses? Nothing will deter her from being an accessory to every type of abortion according to public record. This year she promised: "I will continue to work to ensure a woman's right to choose." This means her energy will be directed to death goals as is her leading the charge to kill the defenseless embryonic persons in ESCR (embryonic stem cell research). She makes the unscientific statement that, "[T]his research has the biblical power to cure." For fuller discussion on the falsity of this statement, the reader is referred to my lengthy essay, "The Catholic Church Supports Stem Cell Research."

It is encouraging to read that her own pastor in San Francisco, Fr. John Malloy SDB released an open letter to Nancy urging her to cease calling herself Catholic and refrain from receiving the Eucharist because he said, "you are fooling yourself and many good Catholics." Would that other Catholic leaders had his courage and faith. The battle lines are drawn between life and death. I trust that John Kennedy was not fully responsible for what he set up. Perhaps in God's mercy his ignorance will be his salvation. Nevertheless, the consequences of his thought have been enormously negative for the nation. In my own mind, I am content that I did not vote for him. Scripture does teach that we are to choose life. Not death. I am content to pray for Jack and Mario and Kerry and Nancy and Ted and Biden and Daschle and Fr Drinan and Leahy and other Catholics who refuse to follow their Church's teaching (read: the Lord's) and who opt rather to destroy.

St. Michael, Archangel, lead us in the Battle for light and truth and life.

On Dawn Eden and Chastity

Written from a woman's point of view, Dawn Eden's 212-page analysis of chastity is a block buster. Even the clever title, *The Thrill of the Chaste: Finding Fulfillment While Keeping Your Clothes On* (Ave Maria Press 2015), boldly challenges the sacred cows of the Second Avenue bar crowd. Perhaps, even those of the Third Avenue bar crowd. The interpersonal fraudulences, the phony conversations so obviously marked by the roving eye searching for a potential contact, the in-authenticities, and most of all, the drab emptiness of the unchaste life are ruthlessly exposed. Her notion of the thrilled life of the chaste is essentially different from the contemporary sad notion of the thrill of the chased.

The hip stereotyping of the chaste ones as frigid, sexually frightened, up tight and boring does not square with her present thinking or her own personal past experience in the hip world. While, on the one hand, she had the healthy and profound desire to marry her Prince Charming who hopefully would treat her as a princess sharing her values, at the same time, she had great fear of rejection as well as intimacy, big time. She had huge urgencies which never seemed to be resolved. She was the one who was always "dumped" (her word). One can wonder and even faintly understand why so many young women, in that painful, confused state, have, in effect, thrown good sense and caution to the winds and hoped that a little sex experience would open the doors to marriage and romantic, eternal love.

She, like so many other young women on the modern scene, might hear the biological clock ticking, be desperately lonely with little to do beyond watching television and getting drunk on weekends. Insert panic into that scenario and one has a recidivistic and insecure way of life. It looks like an emotional merry-go-round pattern which probably ends in the same unfulfilling way. It also sounds close to what the shrink world calls "unconscious depression." She notes (p. 3) that "the most I could hope for, it seemed, was a man who would treat me with 'respect,' but who really wouldn't have any concern for me once we split the tab for breakfast." She describes as "pathetic" the old game where it was just one more uncomfortable morning-after breakfast with her loveless partner oozing with respect (at least what qualifies as respect in the dating world). His "I'll still respect you" line became more than she could bear.

I wonder how any naïve young woman would feel if she heard the locker room talk among young men discussing the broads they recently conquered (they usually use another street term, raunchy and inelegant)? There is little respect in the descriptions of their exploits. Again, on the unconscious level, it is rather disrespect they feel for the girl who gave in. In fact, the morning-after guy is handing out balderdash.[62] It is, on the contrary, goodness which wins real, if grudging, respect. The goodness which vibes out from human beings is powerfully attractive and I suspect that on some level, the modern yearns for the nostalgia of his own lost virtue. Let us face it—in some ways, goodness can be very sexy!

Dawn had thought, incorrectly, that by introducing the sexual component into the relationship, she might control her lover and nudge him a tad toward marriage. But, contrary wise, she writes of her feelings of being trapped and getting none of the goodies promised by the media and popular wisdom. She had the infantile fantasy that merely having sex with him would make him love her. It was once again the age-old myth of the famous non-equation: "Sex equals love."

From my private practice, I recall an interview with a young woman in her mid-thirties, a graduate of a prestigious

Catholic college who enthusiastically slept around looking for love, closeness and, most of all, marriage. Her dominant involvement was with a middle-aged man who loved to roller blade and go to black tie parties but who required a sexual dimension in his relationship with her. She desperately wanted a baby and assumed that her partner would come around to her mode of thinking, especially after a year's tossing in the hay. In a painful counseling session with them, I raised the question of marriage which totally surprised the bon vivant. Not only did he clear the air by surfacing his hip value system which insisted that sex before marriage is far better than after any ceremony, but, with a straight face, he informed the deluded young woman "I don't owe you anything—certainly not marriage." Subsequently she suffered severe emotional reactions, becoming an alcoholic with puffy eyelids and another bewildered modern. How dopey can a young woman be? Or is common sense irrelevant here?

Dawn is too intelligent to irrevocably follow such a tragic regimen. Her intelligence coupled with a gracious turn of God's grace led her to become chaste whereby she has found a joy she never even suspected was available.

How many times, both as priest and psychologist, I have urged young women to follow the law of God and the centuries of healthy human experience. Effectively, that means chastity. Time after time, speaking with some of them, I found it exceedingly difficult to dislodge the notion that chastity is a grim, dour no-no. Some kind of symbolic chastity belt by which all joy is repressed, sexual feelings are inherently evil, affection is taboo, and love is an academic word meant only for intellectual dissection. Chastity on Second Avenue apparently means that life is essentially sad. In other words, the perception on the street is a total distortion. Is this simply an extension of the unspoken law that if I desire something, I should have it? And that I will become neurotic if I am denied my wishes? Is it Second Avenue infantilism?

How does one explain and persuade that chastity is so much more[63] than the adult containment of libidinous drives? How does one illustrate that chastity means feeling interiorly clean and almost electrically alive with the creative juices flowing abundantly? How does one communicate the towering feeling of being on the right side of God? How does one sing of the energy and the vigor that comes with the new self-respect (the running mate of chastity) making one independent of the approval of Second Avenue? How does one proclaim the great feeling of truly enjoying the world and its beauty and not having to be on the hunt for a prospective partner for the night? How does one shout how great it is to jettison the sad eyes and the brittle, empty wit of the hip crowd? How can one articulate the freedom that chastity gives to behold another without attempting possession and suffocation? How can one relate how rejection and intimacy fears have lessened and how self-confidence and self-respect have burgeoned? How to teach the cross of Christ as a resolution for absurdity?

Dawn Eden can answer those questions. And better than most that I have ever read.

But, clearly, this is not just a question of good sense, data, experience, and logic. The unchastity problem stems from fantasy, archaic feelings, rampant urgent longings and biology run amok. If one reviews the reality, women like Dawn don't have to be unchaste. The urge to marry is good and holy as planned by the loving Creator, God Himself. Males and females are drawn to each other in the marvelous design of God. We surely can say, "Vive les XX and XY chromosomes!" The plan is meant for union, not only for the procreation of the human species (not nature's trick to ensure survival) but also for complementarity. The plan is not meant for dead end one-night stands, with the no-strings-attached baloney, nor for eunicoids and unisexuals. Nor for the absurdity of same-sex unions. Only men and women can complete each other and, specifically, help each other to reach holiness in the marital union. This is a good and beautiful plan to which the overwhelming majority of the human race, at least in terms of completion, can subscribe.

Dawn saw that chastity, in fact, improved her chances for a happy marriage, not jeopardized it. She is a petite, pretty, intelligent, witty woman with a slight but charming stammer. She sees now through the lens of chastity that there is no need for her to flirt or bat her eyelashes at some attractive man or to say whatever she thinks he wants to hear. She knows that she is God's own child who loves her and is with her each second of her life. She is a free person. She didn't need a physical makeover, in the fashion of some female politicos who trade horn rimmed glasses for contact lenses, who exchange dowdy clothes and frowsy hairdos for an expensive and relatively acceptable public persona. Dawn needed a spiritual make-over to rescue her from her duping by the irreal.[64]

I heard her discuss her book in a crowded hall recently where young people listened in rapture as she presented chastity—straight, non-sugarcoated, replete with Scripture quotes, theological insights and thoroughly in sync with Pope John Paul II's theology of the body. She spoke (as she writes) of closeness with God through chastity, and its consequent reward of inner peace and self-esteem. In a private discussion with her, she opined that should she write the book over she would make a greater point of promoting chastity as an end—for itself. As valid and powerful as is her thesis that chastity is the way to find one's mate, her expanded point is even more fundamental. Chastity is the integrating virtue that makes sense out of life. It is a key to inner peace and to that elusive treasure: contentment.

Her book is in my consulting office where I have already recommended it to patients, men as well as women, young and old, hip and square. As stated above, it is a blockbuster.

Old Priests and the Mass

Early every morning a group of old priests (usually about ten) meet in a beautiful little chapel on Manhattan's West Side to concelebrate the Holy Sacrifice of the Mass. They range in age from a relatively young seventy-two to a mature ninety-two. They use wheelchairs, walkers, canes, or they shuffle, painful step by painful step, to worship their God and to confront their mortality. Their infirmities and medical experience include bypass heart surgery, myocardial infarctions, crippling arthritis, TKR (total knee replacements), cancer, vertigo, rotator cuff repairs and cataract removal. Almost all suffer from some degree of deafness, moderate to severe. More than occasionally, their brain synapses fire improperly. They are white haired and gray haired and very bald. They, *laudatores temporis acti*,[65] are men living long past their eras which were the Great Depression, the Great War of 1941-45, Bing Crosby and Frances Langford.

The Mass is in silence with no distraction from guitars or nasal rendition of New Age hymnody which most of them find not only unfamiliar but disturbing. Before the Mass, they gather silently in the darkened chapel before the Lord in the Blessed Sacrament reaching for the recommended frame of mind enjoined on them at their ordination so long ago. "Be like that which you handle." The sanctuary lamp flickers in the darkness with no sound but the hiss of the radiators which warms in winter or the hum of the A/C in summer which shields them from the brutal New York humidity.

I, myself, am one of these old men. I join them at Mass so that I, under God, might draw some strength, resolve and faith from their simple, uncomplicated devotion. I knew them all when they were young and energetic, when they had the proverbial tiger by the tail. I knew them when they were full of vibrancy and wit. I remember when they were so popular, people would wait for days to see them, as if they were a religious neurosurgeon with incredible skill to heal. Now, for example, one of these, a former clerical star, has, after Mass is completed, only three things to do to fill his day: Breakfast, lunch and dinner.

No longer do these creaky old clerics receive the wide-eyed adulation and admiration of their active younger days. No longer do their phones ring requesting time with the great man. No one seeks him out for advice or affirmation or guidance. The applause is gone. There are no longer great crowds hanging on his every utterance making him feel like a king of the universe. In fact, the lives of these old priests are quiet, sometimes boring and lonely. They watch television which saturates them with insipid sometimes insulting shows. They read newspapers for hours, carefully noting the obituaries and ultimately the advertisements (with no intent to buy anything). They have, like so many others fellow humans, grown old. This means a loss of power, independence, control, opportunities for mobility and fun. This means peril to their self-esteem and their confidence. Always it can border on depression and unhappiness for the man of God.

One of them who died at ninety-five used to lament that no one sought his advice about the recruiting process for his community. He had been an active Director of Vocations in the past, a war hero, decorated for bravery, and involved in four terrifying invasions in Europe. He, in a fit of pique, once said to me, "Why don't they ever ask me my opinion?" I, now unhappy in retrospect with my words, replied: "Because they don't care about your opinion." Though inelegant, this response was probably correct. That is simply the way it is. We are all the same and most probably we acted identically in our own youth.

Against such a sad but realistic background one can appreciate somewhat why these ancients are so faithful and involved in the daily Mass. While it is a formidable and concrete expression of the human need for community and the yearning for interaction with other congenial human beings, the meaning of the daily meeting is far more profound than the merely natural. Yes, obviously concelebrating the daily Mass is far more bonding than watching late night TV together or even perfunctory breaking bread at a common table. With a kind of Gospel spin[66] on it, we could say that the factual pagan can develop community at a sports bar watching the Jets and guzzling beer with the guys. Nothing wrong with that but hardly comparable to what happens when a group of priests, old or young, gather to participate in Calvary and the Last Supper. Obviously, these priests see something.

The bonding at the Mass stems from a common belief. These old men, soon to face their God for their personal judgment, believe that they are actually representing Mount Calvary and the crucifixion and death of Jesus, their Master Who, in fact, is God Himself. They believe that they, as other Christs, ordained as such, are instruments of something so ineffable that it escapes definition. After years of study, reading, listening, praying, intellectualizing, they cannot really understand but only believe that they instrumentally (as *in persona Christi* priests) bring down Christ Himself on that very altar where they stand. Not in the ordinary sense of Jesus among us by Baptism, prayer or good works, but in this unique presence of the Lord we call the Blessed Sacrament.

A friend of mine, a hard-nosed labor negotiator, told me as we were sharing some pasta e fagioli and Italian bread, that should I say the words of consecration over the bread there, he would get down on his knees in the restaurant—before all other diners—and worship Christ in the Eucharist. Without assessing his personal eucharistic theology, he does reflect that *sensus fidelium*[57] about this tremendous mystery which so dominates the lives of old priests. He also reflects how these old priests see the Mass and themselves.

They believe, by their very words, that a change takes place. That which is just bread or wine now becomes the actual Body and Blood of Jesus Himself. He, the Master, is there before these old chaps through their words. Theologians try to explain this by fancy thinking using, for example, the term, transubstantiation, change of substance and not of externals. But it is the faith which illumines the heart. Believe it or not. That is what they believe and that is why they are there day after day. Hot days or freezing days. Every day. They are there to meet the Master in a way simply not possible in any other manner. In the Mass, a sacrifice of the Lord for all of us, the old priests receive consolation and comfort, reassurance of His love for them and His gratitude to them for their years of difficult burdens for His sake. This Mass experience cannot be replaced. I recall the famous Protestant preacher, William Sloane Coffin, remarking "There is no substitute for the Mass." Preaching, good works, counseling, teaching, administering, organizing are all good things but none can equal the Mass. Dr. Coffin lamented, however, about Catholic priests, "If those guys could only preach." He may be right on that but good preaching without the Mass can hardly compete.

But is it only old age that makes these old guys so faithful and loyal every morning? The older priest does notice that apparently his younger confreres do not share his view of the Mass. He asks why don't the young guys show up for this concelebration? I wonder myself on those cold, cold mornings when my joints ache and I want to stay under the warm covers, why should I, at eight-six, get up? The young guys don't. Do they know something I don't? They are probably smarter and better educated than I, so why don't they show up? How come they say Mass only when they are obliged to? How come Bishop

A. Vaughan, rector of the New York Seminary, instructed his young priests to say Mass every day and not just attend it? How come they say Mass only if there is an assembly present? How come they disagree with Pope John Paul II who in his encyclical *De Eucharistia* # 31 encourages priests to say Mass daily—even if there is no one else present? How come old priests believe private Masses are not private at all but public before the very court of heaven with God the father presiding? With all the angels and saints? With Our Blessed Lady smiling on the priest? Is this a question of catechesis? Or is it a reflection of a different kind of faith about the Mass?

I don't know. But I know that these old guys love to say Mass daily because it is the one solid, changeless, meaningful love we have. Being old is tough enough but to be without the one ultimate support would be, in the words of the kids I knew on the street many years ago, "plain bananas."

Say Either Yea or Nay—The Nauseating of Christ

"I wish you were either cold or hot. So, because you are lukewarm, neither hot nor cold, I will vomit [spit, spue, spew][68] *you out of my mouth."* Rev. 3:16

It is a contemporary truism to say that we live in a litigious society which is ever searching for any possible chance to sue. Attorneys nearly salivating at the wide range of prospects, look for the quick and easy buck. In such a threatening legal climate, a restrained and super cautious expression of one's values and ideas is understandable, especially if one espouses an unpopular cause. Augmented by a near hysterical need to avoid trampling on almost[69] anyone's sensitivities, modern discourse is heavily characterized by ambiguity, circumlocution and overuse of the word alleged.

The high-level magazine *New Oxford Review* ("NOR") published an item concerning a Catholic bishop in Colorado who stated that from henceforth he will make no comment on the behavior of homosexuals lest he might offend someone's sensibilities. The editors of *NOR* rightly confronted the bishop wondering whether such a constricted verbal prison might not logically inhibit him from commenting on any kind of sinful behavior. They asked whether such timidity would not factually reduce him to the level of a weak and ineffectual spiritual leader.

However, speaking plainly without ambiguity and with courage does exact a price. Another Catholic bishop in Canada who writes a regular newspaper essay, often simply stating (without festooning) the basic Catholic teaching on sexuality, was threatened with jail time by the previous prime minister. His offense was to be categorized a hate crime. If the prime minister's viewpoint were universal, every government would need many more jails since this crime is regularly committed by every loyal Catholic teacher of the faith throughout the world. Fortunately for everyone, the threatening prime minister was not reelected, and his successor adopted a more adult view of freedom of speech and expression. In some societies, however, telling the truth puts one at great risk. Following Christ's injunction, quoted above, might exact a great price from many Christians.

A particularly debasing motivation for shading the truth is the insatiable desire in some human beings to be liked by everyone. This is obviously an illusion more suited to the dreamy fantasies of adolescents than adults. Some such emotionally retarded adults are devastated if someone dislikes them. Their criterion for living becomes, not truth, but the quicksand of being liked. It was said of a popular politician that he agreed with the last person he spoke to. He was exceedingly well liked because he said what he thought the other wished to hear. He had little integrity but plenteous admiration.

While the modern fear of a retribution is more intense, there has always been some kind of watching your tongue in human history. I remember the well-known custom in Ireland of never answering a direct question. Better, we were told, to answer with a question, lest your answer be used somehow against you. So, when I was seeking a relative in Ireland, I stopped an old gent in Cork asking him if he knew where my cousin lived. He narrowed his eyes, took out his pipe and said, "Now what would you be wantin' to see her for, I wonder?" The "I wonder" was said with the famous Cork corkscrew tonality as it phonetically spiraled up and up. Such caution was apparently a carryover from the old penal days when the Irish were terribly persecuted by an occupying foreign power. It was a question of always being on your guard. Don't ever let them know what you really think. Sometimes paranoia is understandable.

It is somewhat similar in the accepted custom of illegals lying after they have crossed one of our borders, the southern one, for example. Better to lie because they might use it against you and deport you if you tell the whole story. Is it not common knowledge that the American Indian became highly suspicious and untrusting of white men because of the double speak used against him? "White man speak with forked tongue" was a well-used expression in our western states.

In contemporary society, it is rampant. Recently, in a publicly televised debate between various candidates for nomination to the presidency, the question was asked of all of them: "What is your view of *Roe v. Wade* relative to overturning it?" One of the leading candidates, a self-confessed Catholic, replied: "If it is overturned, it is okay. If it is not overturned, it is okay." Nowhere did he indicate to the country what he actually thought about *Roe v. Wade*. The Catholic faith specifically teaches that abortion is intrinsically evil and that Catholics must do what they can to protect innocent life, for example, the unborn child. This politician would not take a position and preferred to take the middle road, i.e., the lukewarm one mentioned by the Lord. It was reminiscent of the noted television commentator who, when asked about the outcome of a troublesome situation, replied: "Well, it might be right and it might be wrong." He cashed big checks for such intellectual bravery.

Such nauseating evasion obviously covers not only the religious but also the political landscape. Some years ago, a Catholic woman was running for a very high political office but, for election purposes, wiggled a position on abortion whereby she tried to have her feet on both sides. Worse than the evader mentioned above, this woman misrepresented the Church's teaching and attributed her liberal position to some priest advisors who assured her, she said, that her position was truly Catholic. She dismissed the religious leadership of the local cardinal archbishop who insisted on publication of true Catholic teaching. She lost the election possibly because of her shocking religious bifurcation.

Such refusal to take a clear Catholic position on the part of Catholics is unbelievable and discouraging to the millions of devout believers. To learn that Catholic senators and congressmen vote in favor of partial birth abortion utterly confuses moral people. The weaseling practice to append "so-called" to the term partial birth is further confounding. It is eminently clear that this barbarous practice is the dismemberment of a living child. Is it that these people cannot face the fact of this murder themselves? Are they trying to cover it over in their own consciences? One thing we do know. This usage of "so called" falls under the nausea described by Christ. It is a refusal to call something for what it is. Our people have a right to know what God asks. Ambiguity is not helpful. Clarity is.

The recently deceased Federal Court Judge Richard Casey closely questioned an abortionist in an investigation of the legality of partial-birth abortion. He asked the man who had performed many of these procedures whether the baby felt any pain during the dismemberment. As the limbs are being pulled from the torso of the child, is there any suffering inflicted on the child? The professional killer replied that he never thought of it. It never entered his mind. Really? After hundreds of these procedures? Or is it that he unconsciously knows what he is doing and even censures himself? Ducking the meaning of one's actions and their consequences falls under the thundering condemnation of the Lord. Penumbras and emanations are proper material for discussions in the Supreme Court. They do not belong where the sunlit leadership of Jesus illuminates.

The choice demanded by the Lord clearly involves suffering. One cannot take both sides of a fundamental moral issue where there is only one side. To attempt the lukewarm describes the repulsive practice of engaging in the oxymoronic[70] which is implied in the Scripture. Lukewarm means trying to put opposites together so that everyone is content with the result. One of the worst and most dishonest I have ever seen is the oxymoronic title of "Catholics for a Free Choice," the organization with no members, run for years by the now retired Frances Kissling. The use of the word Catholic linked with abortion (choice as euphemism) is an intellectual confliction. It was as if one could be a practicing Catholic and simultaneously, acceptably engage in abortion and the like.

I had the privilege of meeting the lead bishop of all the Protestant churches of the Church of Ireland when I was chairing a graduate division at Iona college. He was charming and pleasant, extremely nice to be around. He spoke easily, met all of us with grace, gentleness and ease while wearing a huge red vest-like front for his clerical collar. No wonder we all liked him so much. But he had a powerful tool to affect this popularity. He never gave a real opinion about anything. No matter what was being discussed or opined, he would reply "I know, I know." It was done with charm and an engaging smile, but no one knew where he stood on difficult matters. Is that the road to political or ecclesiastical success? Don't ruffle feathers. Be very agreeable. Don't ever disagree. Smile. Don't take strong positions. Go for the gray area in everything.

It is easy to understand the accurate and careful reporting of many people who hesitate to make statement because they do not have data at hand. But the one who fears to state his views lest he be punished by social isolation or job loss or physical punishment is something else. It is easy to understand the refusal of someone to answer a specious question which is posed, like the Pharisees, to embarrass another. Yet part of the Christian life is to be courageous and truthful. It is truly difficult so to live yet we believe that the Lord gives the strength to be open and trusting knowing that He is with us always. When we live as He requests, the inner feeling is clean and relaxed. I have nothing to fear. My Lord my God is with me. My God stands by me, I place all my trust in Him. May it come to pass in the modern Catholic. It is desperately needed.

On Narcissism, or Why Doesn't the World See How Marvelous I Am?

In a recent public lecture, an eminent New York City cleric, while musing on the famous John Donne quip "No man is an island," perceptively opined that today everyone is an island. He suggested that the modern is so turned in on himself that he becomes the center of all things. Everything is measured in terms how things affect him personally. He is deep into peak experiences which might be rollerblades, trendy restaurants, or BMWs. Because of his involvement with himself, he is increasingly alienated and lonely in the super-busy megapolis which is "Today."

Despite the numerous gadgets and technical toys he may have, the modern is often markedly depressed and unhappy. Why is this? The Catholic psychiatrist, Conrad Baars, has suggested that the culprit may very well be narcissism, the modern-day disease. Quite correctly, I think, the twentieth century has been called the age of narcissism with its intense self-centeredness and hedonistic questing.

The term narcissism comes from an old myth wherein a handsome youth, Narcissus, falls passionately in love with his own image reflected in a pool. Because of his preoccupation with himself, he is unable to hear anyone else say to him, "I love you." He ultimately pines away and dies. He, however, leaves behind a recognizable blueprint for an unhappy psyche, which has been seduced by an infatuating self-love and which is accompanied by a tragic unrequited hunger for the ideal lover whom he can never find. Contemporary psychology uses the term to describe a vain preoccupation with self or a preening self-centeredness, even slipping sometimes into the auto erotic. The usual triad is vanity, exhibitionism, and arrogant ingratitude.

Look everybody—here I am! Look, everybody, watch me perform! Why should I be grateful? The world owes me. I deserve it all. And everybody has to like me! I am teed off if they don't pay attention to me and appreciate me! Take care of me, first!

How many times I, like so many others, have seen the juvenile behavior of a fifty-year-old teenager demanding attention, grabbing the social spotlight, or raging because of a perceived slight. As one such narcissist told me once, "Say anything about me when I am not here, but don't ignore me when I am here." Perhaps such behavior stems from a deep and underlying sense of insecurity. Perhaps, the culprit was poor mothering. Or a poor sense of self-esteem and self-value. Or perhaps it is as Austrian-born American psychoanalyst Heinz Kohut taught in 1977. It is a failure in normal development of the earliest internal images of self and significant others. And there is always the real enemy. Inordinate pride. Or put differently, it means that the narcissist needs some deep instruction and guidance on the meaning of the basic virtue of humility. There are clear parameters of reality, even if unclear to the narcissist, which were established by God Himself. If the Lord's reality is not seen, personal chaos necessarily results. It is absurd to believe that I am the center of the universe. Yet, in effect, this is the emotional position of the one who suffers (and inflicts suffering on others) because of a narcissistic orientation. He doesn't seem to know that God is the center, not the human "I."

What impels, for example, the high-powered A-type personality, the business tycoon, the educator, the cinema star, the cleric to rush to booze in times of stress? From my own practice dealing with such people, it seems to me that there is a real correlation between heavy drinking and a subjective belief that he is not being sufficiently appreciated, loved, or acknowledged. What drives the seductive and insatiable behavior of the person who is competing for the affection of the world? Even his own circumscribed world? There seems to be a huge need to be constantly reassured that he is loveable or capable or appreciated. Narcissism or the exaggerated sense of self-importance might well be the villain.

If, in an earlier age, society believed that we were all responsible to some degree for each other in that every word, deed, thought[71] and omission somehow rippled out and affected everyone we met, the today theme is more, "I don't want to get involved" or "Let George do it" or "I got mine, Mac."

Today, it is almost axiomatic to hold that each of us has the right (by some kind of cosmic, consensual dynamic) to say or do or not to do or think or desire or ignore—anything we want, whatever we want—regardless of any impact on others. It is almost enough justification to say merely that I desire something to make it acceptable. If I want it, I should have it— otherwise I will be damaged emotionally. The old fashioned but healthy principles of waiting for the fulfillment of one's needs with self-restraint and of understanding the notion of delayed gratification, seem quaint and out of step. There is a powerful demon in our midst which demands, not delayed gratification, but instant gratification. Despite the bleeding-heart human-family drumbeat and the pious lip service (usually done on the high-flown abstract level mode[72]) there is a widespread culture of frightening self-centeredness in our land. We suspect, in agreement with Baars, that the damaging enemy is narcissism.

As always, however, there are the beautiful social pockets of altruism which reject selfishness and inspire others to the doing of the good. For example, where we have legal support for abortion for those who loathe the inconvenience of birthing and rearing a child, we also have the multitudes of women who unselfishly and lovingly give life and love to little kids who will live forever. Generous and unselfish people? See the Sisters of

Life who lovingly take care of the losers and the unwanted. See the Franciscan Friars of Benedict Groeschel with their youthful, enthusiastic and generous care of the poor, the unwashed and angry poor. See the many volunteers for soup kitchens, nursing homes and meals on wheels. We have the candy stripers in hospitals and high school students who read to the blind. We have the Habitat for Humanity. We have the young undergraduates who pray outside abortuaries, risking insult and arrest because they care for others.

So even though Baars is probably right, not everyone is an island. There is great hope under God for altruism because there are good people in our world and God's grace is ever available. Nevertheless, Baars is right in positing that something has happened to the Western Judeo-Christian soul to make so many of us turn back into ourselves where things are evaluated, basically and concretely, in terms of me. In my eighties, I was saddened (and even shaken) to note a news story about my old alma mater, NYU, in Greenwich Village. A survey taken shortly after 9/11 indicated that a large sample of the student body avowed that, even in extreme war circumstances, they had no intention to serve their country. The common theme was, "Let someone else do it." And "I have to take care of my own career."

While in my youth (the Pearl Harbor era), there were some scattered gold-brick types who personified the let-George-do-it mentality, the overwhelming majority of the population was eager—in some way—to give of themselves to help others. Even to the point of serving in the military. Today we have truly magnificent volunteers in the service, female as well as male, who are willing to donate some years of their lives (even under very dangerous conditions) to protect God's good world. However, their numbers are comparatively few.

Narcissism is hardly confined to military service. It is everywhere. In families. In schools. In the pulpit (with the built-in stage for exhibitionism with the startling success of many preachers and evangelists). In offices. Extraordinarily in the theatre. In politics. In the athletic world. In short, wherever you find human beings, you will find selfishness, self-magnification and self-involvement. And all human beings are flawed and self-concerned because of a great aboriginal calamity that occurred long ago in the beginning of the human race. Catholics call it original sin. As Captain McNeill told his brilliant, bald Lieutenant in an episode of the TV series *Kojak*, "Theo, this is an imperfect world and I have a lifetime membership in it." So, of course, our concern is more with degree than with kind. Obviously, narcissism exists in all of us but hopefully might be minimized for everyone's benefit. But what is possible?

Some analysts suggest that narcissists contribute a measure of sparkle and wonder to life and should we restore them to the elusive criterion of normality, we would lose their electric contribution to our world. Such advisors counsel that we should accept these persons as they are, love them and appreciate whatever great things they actually do. A colleague of mine suggests that, with an elastic concept of normal, they should be considered normal if they can keep their abnormals to a minimum. Nevertheless, narcissists are not as happy as they seem. They often feel empty and frustrated because of their unfulfilled longings. Psychotherapy is marvelous up to a point but is certainly limited since, by a Catholic definition, it merely clears away the path for further and higher growth. Counseling and therapy should be vestibule work. The real answer, as implied above, is in the spiritual world.

How to proceed? Can I get my narcissist to want to grow out of his misery? Can I get him to pray to Jesus for help? And to the Holy Spirit for enlightenment? Can I introduce to him the concept and later the effect of the cross of Jesus? And its meaning and its liberty? How can I help him see that there are others in the world, often far more destitute (which can take many forms) than he? How do I get him to see that his glass, like everyone else, is half full and is usually right under his nose as he keeps looking for greener fields? How can I help him to be content (not smug) with his life? How can I help him understand the joy of empathy wherein he might see things through another's eyes? How can I open to him the joyful glorious feeling of helping others? How can I get him to see and feel the profundity of gratitude? How do I get him to relish the simple things of life, the walking, the smelling of the rose, the feel of rain on his face, the beauty in so many things, the presence of God? How do I get him to learn the great art of offering it up? The art of freedom from others' approval? The art of knowing that ultimately only God's approval matters?

How do I help him see the suicidal results of living in the entitlement mode? How do I get him to sense—even remotely—that God, His Father, loves him with an implacable love even though he is often such a complete schlep? How do I get him to see that home runs are not necessarily what make people happy, but rather simple contentment with the deal given them by the Lord of life? Bottom line, how do I get him to appreciate reality and its limitations? Or in my terms, how do I get him to see, not only by the aha phenomenon, so beloved by shrinks, but also by the eyes of faith that he has value—eternally—proven by his Lord dying for him in a terrible, incredibly painful way? This is the humility we all need. The truth of ourselves not only with our plusses and minuses but with our beauty before God.

Such idealism! Yet that is the goal. If you know how to implement these ideals as stated, please instruct me. Meanwhile, I shall pray that the narcissism we all share will be, as my colleague suggested, kept to a minimum.

About the Author

Hi to everyone who might reach me! I am an old timer WWII type!

My Mother and Father were Vaudevillians and I was a classic "dirty neck kid" from San Juan Hill in West Side Manhattan. Psychologist and bridge player. Old time Television and radio career. NBC, ABC and CBS. Love my Faith and laughing. Retired police chaplain. Love to talk with others who agree or otherwise. Half Irish and half Jewish (Russian) but ALL Catholic. Swimmer and former basketball player.

I'm also the oldest living Paulist Father!

Learn more about Fr. Lloyd at: www.frjameslloyd.com

Endnotes

[1] McGraw-Hill (January 1, 1980).

[2] His word and so appropriate in the 1890's for profound friendship.

[3] The acronym for The North American Man/Boy Love Association.

[4] *Wallace v. Jaffree*, 472 U.S.38, 107.

[5] V. Munoz, "Establishing Free Exercise," *First Things*, Dec. 2003.

[6] *Annals of Congress*, 914 (1789).

[7] *Everson v. Bd. of Ed.*, 330 US, 1,3 (1947_).

[8] *The Recorder*, Dec. 27. 1993.

[9] Or am I speaking of mankind in general? Might all groups of males be broken down in a similar way?

[10] "[F]eigning of beliefs, feelings or virtues that one does not hold or possess; insincerity." *Dictionary* of Houghton, Mifflin Co.

[11] Courage is a Catholic apostolate formed to assist same-sex attracted persons (SSA) to pursue chastity and holiness in the Roman Catholic style.

[12] Hendra, Tony, *Father Joe: The Man Who Saved My Soul* (Random House, 2004), p. 73.

[13] *Ibid.*, p.117.

[14] *Ibid.*, p.197.

[15] *Ibid.*, p.185.

[16] Quote by Meister Eckhart, https://www.goodreads.com/quotes/7818215-when-god-laughs-at-the-soul-and-the-soul-laughs.

[17] Hendra, Tony, *Father Joe: The Man Who Saved My Soul*, p. 133.

[18] It is hilarious to observe that Dan Brown features an Opus Dei "monk" in his book. Opus Dei has no monks at all. It was just made up to fill out the fantasy of the author.

[19] Available from the National Marriage Project, Rutgers—the State University of New Jersey. 25 Bishop Place, New Brunswick, NJ 08901-1181.

[20] The caveat: cohabitating couples living for a short and immediate prelude to marriage can be the exception providing one or both partners have not cohabited with someone else or brought children into the relationship.

[21] Same-sex attraction (SSA) is a modern term used to describe the sexual tendency towards one's own sex. It is thought to be more respectful than homosexual in that SSA regards the person as ordered while his tendency is disordered. The term gay has more of a pervasive sense to it, moving the person to equate his personhood with this tendency. Such an equation is rejected by the Catholic Church.

[22] To New York Priests' Senate, May 2006.

[23] *Catalyst*; June 2006.

24   *Oxford University Press*, 2003.

25   This can mean any kind of sexual behavior exclusively reserved for husbands and wives in marriage. Catholicism does not accept any definition of marriage other than that between a male and a female as defined in Genesis and Scripture in general.

26   `A situation which has been a source of deprivation and even resentment for me. I was never forbidden by my mother's family, only my father's. This can be explained by the experiences of my Jewish grandparents in Russia/Poland relative to the brutal pogroms.

27   He sings as a Cantor in his own synagogue and is deeply involved in its activities. He sees his work at Iona and his friendship with me, at least partially, as a witness and spokesman for the Jewish world.

28   The title Irish Christian Brothers was subsequently changed to Congregation of Christian Brothers as a more accurate reflection of the ethnic makeup of the more recent vocations to the Community. CFC is the present official sign after each brother's name.

29   When one got on the inside one learned that they were called monks.

30   Br. Tom Perry entered the classroom each morning thusly greeting us in French with a pronounced Irish accent.

31   Indeed Ireland no longer supplies recruits as of the old days. Irish Vocations are almost nonexistent. It is India, New Guinea, Africa and what was known as the mission area which keeps the Congregation alive. The present Brother General or leader is from India.

32   In fact, years later, as the Director of Pastoral Counseling at Iona College, I became the first priest to become an associate brother, entitling me to add CFC to my name.

33   He demanded in his scholarship class that everyone who took the Regents exam in solid geometry, get 100 percent on the exam. This was passing to him. I who could hardly add, under his leadership, aced the exam with 100 percent. His secret was check and check and check your work. Repetition was his answer.

34   Sometimes he called himself "Hillary" after a great saint. I prefer for esthetic reasons to use Hilaire since the other resonates an unpleasant note relative to a political figure.

35   I note that in the First World War the Pope refused to bless armaments which are clearly meant to destroy.

36   The in-crowd claim that the United States is next on his agenda.

37   https://clarionproject.org/films/obsession/#

38   The priest scandal largely involved homosexual behaviors, not pederastic ones. The media continues to refer to the problem as if it were about pre-pubescent children,. It was largely about teenaged males, not females and not children of either sex. Homosexual priests were responsible for approximately four out of every five cases of molestation reported over a period of sixty years. This, in itself, is non-objective reporting.

39   "Putting Abuse in Context," Applewhite, Monica, *America* (Sept.25, 2006).

40   "Needs" are defined by the superior intelligence of media.

41   There are certain radical groups within the Catholic Church, including some with-it priests and religious who, finding chaste celibacy too difficult, lobby for sexual rights.

42   Calumny means outright lies about another human being thereby ruining that person's good name and possibly career.

43   Obviously, this is in reference to false charges. Homosexual (or otherwise) priests who molest others are liable themselves before God.

44   One can use the masculine gender in almost every case since there have been, up to now zero allegations of priests molesting, for example, altar girls who are now serving at the altar for about twelve years. The clear inference is that priest molesters are usually not interested in females.

45   Dream recall is highly criticized for its unscientific and unreliable procedure. Cf APA position on this matter.

46   Wearing turtleneck type garb allows priests to get out from under the social expectation of Catholic laypersons. It allows the priest to be one of the boys more easily. Some few priests feel the guilt of the pressure of priesthood and find relief in pretending to be laymen.

47   In my years of teaching graduate students (nuns, brothers and priests), I was amazed at the common rationalization for sexual acting out. So often it was called natural behavior or necessary human development. Nowhere was there mention of the commitment of the vows. I was told either that mortal sin was very difficult ever to commit or that our new insights of morality made such behavior understandable.

48   Tolerance of homosexuals within the order and departure from care of the poor were the alleged reasons to split and form a new community.

49   Some Catholic moralists hold smoking is immoral since it is such a clear hazard to health. Some similarly argue that prize fighting or boxing is forbidden since it so often damages participants. I have heard analogous assessment of football where so many players are seriously injured.

50   Does this imply greater expectation of further vast funding? To whom does this money go? Cui bono? Who is benefiting financially from all the lobbying? Do big pharmaceutical firms have totally altruistic interest in ESCR (Embryonic Stem Cell Research)?

51   George Daley, stem cell researcher at Children's Hospital in Boston admitted that his optimistic prediction (relative to cloned tissue) has "yet to be proven."

52   Stem Cell Research, Cloning and Human Embryos: Family Research Council, Washington D.C. 2005.

53   It was rumored that one movie type deliberately omitted his symptom controlling medication so that he could be filmed in a commercial advocating stem cell research. With hands trembling and head rolling he

masterfully pleaded that the funding should be allotted to research (it seemed with implication of ESCR)—apparently implying that such finding would quickly clear up his and others' disease.

54 In the Catholic system, conscience must be informed by God's revelation and the teachings of Christ's Church. Deciding for oneself means moral relativism—each man for himself. One might consult the writings of Pope John Paul II on conscience formation and the 1998 statement of US bishops on *The Gospel of Life* (Pauline Books and Media 1995).

55 Jack opposed Federal aid to parochial schools and the appointment of an ambassador to the Vatican, positions he had previously held. Why did he reverse his positions?

56 Peggy Noonan reports that an agnostic friend of hers explains the existence of war (and presumably other manmade evils) by saying, "…because there is something wrong within us." JFK didn't seem to understand this.

57 "Inalienable" in the *Declaration of Independence* means "from God." It cannot be taken away by a majority vote.

58 Many commentators consider that the term pro-choice is a kind of cop-out or euphemism to avoid the blunt and more truthful term pro-abortion.

59 Do not all politicians and lobbyists try to influence others to their point of view? Is this imposing? Catholics use moral suasion, to try to alert others to the revealed will of the Lord. This is not imposition.

60 Supreme Court Judge John Noonan (Calif.) has, in the past, seriously questioned the validity of such Janus-like, two headed, cognitive behavior as have many other serious thinkers.

61 Celebrate Life March, April 2007.

62 There is a more colorful street term which accurately describes such behavior which I hesitate to use, in the name of good taste.

63 Chastity certainly does contain sexual behavior as such, but does believe that full, passionate, joyful, physical expression belong only in marriage between a man and united lawfully so. There are no exceptions. In marriage, sexual expression is holy and highly to be encouraged. Vatican II taught the two purposes of sex are: 1) procreation—obvious, and 2) "consolation" of the couple. God smiles on their sexual love.

64 Not unreal, but irreal or counter reality.

65 They praise the past. Cyberspace, iPods and the "voice of the faithful" do not interest them.

66 Even the pagans do that!

67 The sense of the faithful—an instinct for theological truth. Different from the "voice of the faithful" which tends more toward political control rather than Catholic devotion.

68 Some interpretations use the more colorful "I will begin to vomit thee out of My mouth."

69 Except Catholicism. See Philip Jenkins in his book, *The New Anti-Catholicism: The Last Acceptable Prejudice.*

70   Oxymoronic: the attempt to reconcile contradictory concepts within the same word or phrase.

71   Contemporary psychotherapy, unconsciously or not, underscores in a subtle way the Jesus observation that merely lusting for another without external actions is certainly a form of behavior which has consequences.

72   It is usually safer to espouse causes away from the actual site problem. The armchair and the martini make for comfortable and uninvolved social indignation. The limousine liberal in Chappaqua is a good example.